Jump Up
Phonics 1

International Linguistics Research Institute

Jump Up Phonics 1

First Published May, 2008
Sixth Printing January, 2018

Published by: English Department of ILR Institute
Illustrator: Lee gyeongtaek
Publisher: Hwang Uigwon

51-18 Wonhyo-ro 1ga, Yongsan-gu, Seoul, Korea
Tel: 02-704-0900 Fax: 02-703-5117
Homepage: www.bookcamp.co.kr

Editor: Kim Yonghyeon, Moon Seongwon, Paek Hyeyoung
Cover Designer: Min Sunyoung
Designer: Min Sunyoung
Published by ILR Institute
Distributed by Joheungeul Publishing Co., Ltd.
ISBN: 978-89-5911-097-1

Jump Up
Phonics 1

International Linguistics Research Institute

CONTENTS

Aa
Bb
Cc
Dd
Mm
Nn
Oo
Pp
Qq
Rr
Ss

Ee
Ff
Gg
Hh
Ii
Ll
Kk
Jj
Tt
Uu
Vv
Ww
Zz
Yy
Xx

Unit 1 Alphabet Aa Bb Cc

An ant has an apple.
A bear has a big ball.
A cat has a crown and a candy.
What pretty animals!

Listen and repeat. track 02

A a

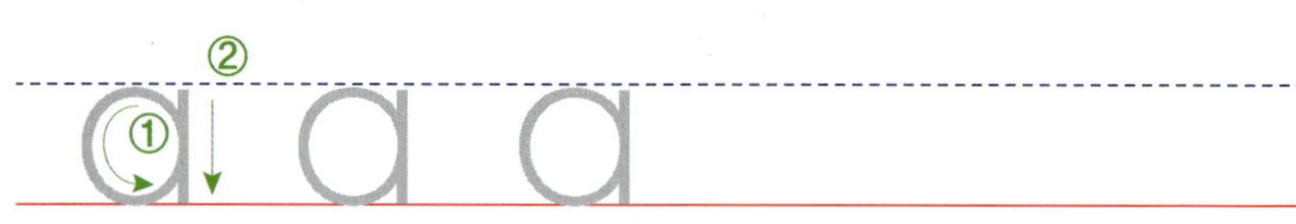

B b

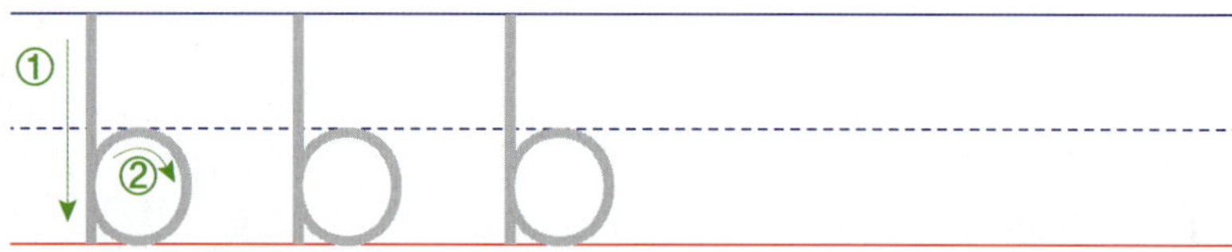

C c

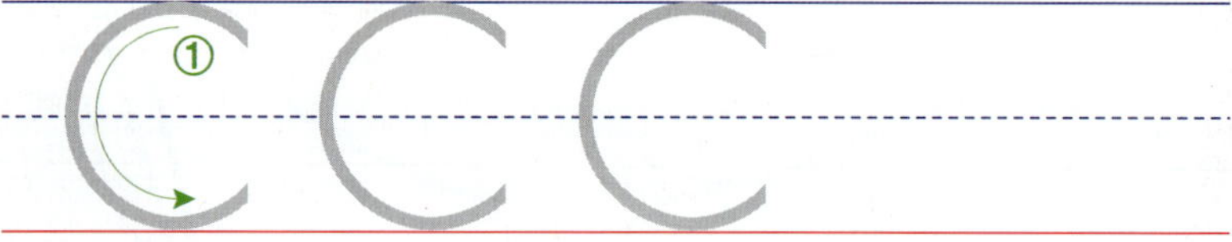

NEW WORDS

Listen, point and repeat. **track 03**

A a

ant

apple

animal

B b

bear

big

ball

C c

cat

crown

candy

Listen and check the beginning sound letter. track 04

1 
a b c

2 
a b c

3 
a b c

4 

a b c

5 
a b c

6 
a b c

Color the same sound with the same color.

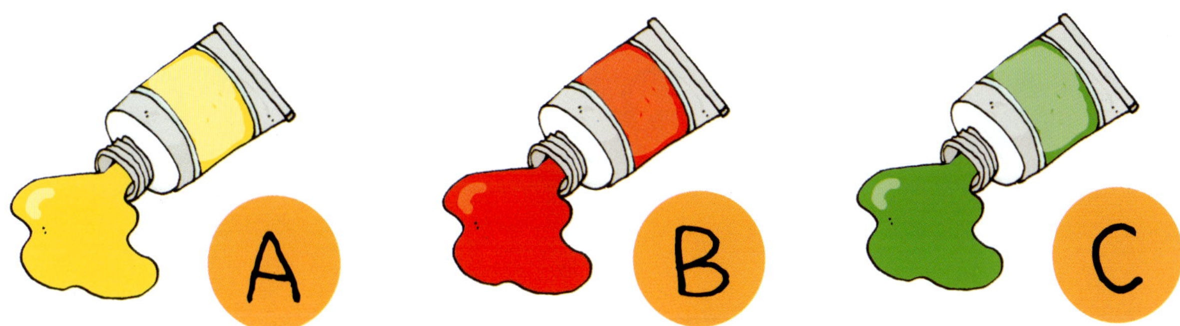

PRACTICE - READ

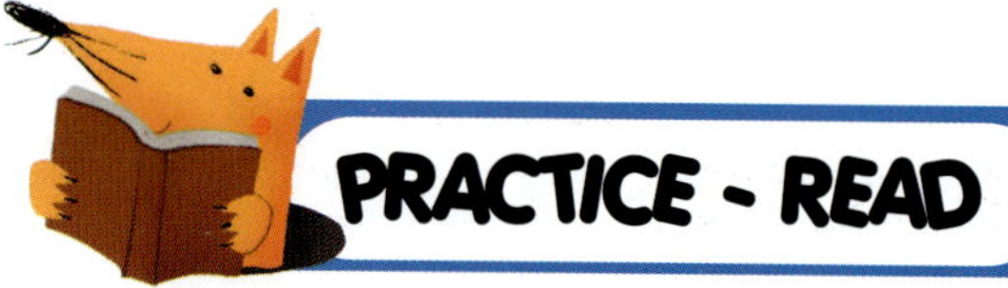

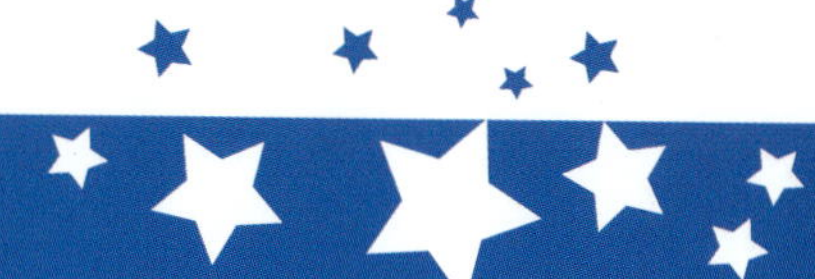

Circle the correct picture.

1. A a

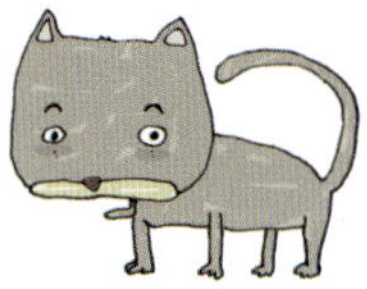 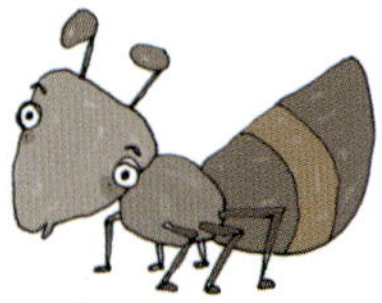 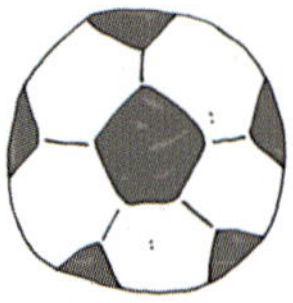

2. C c

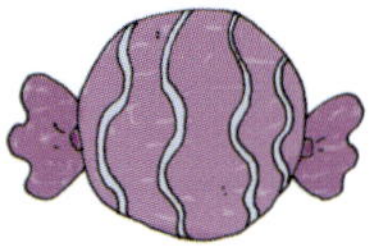 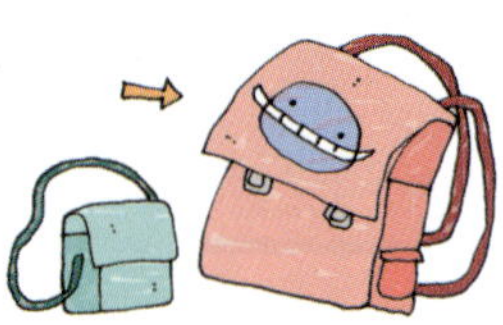 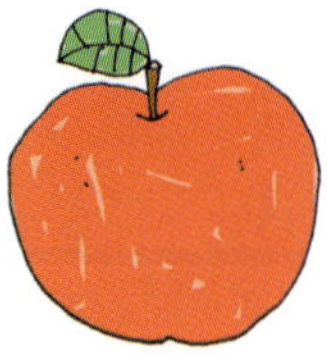

3. B b

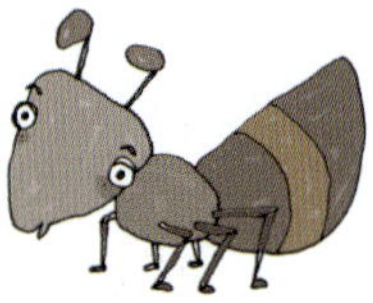 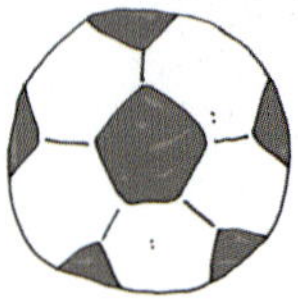 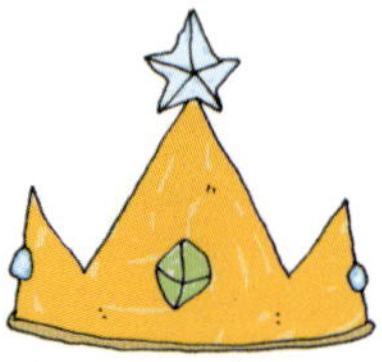

4. B b

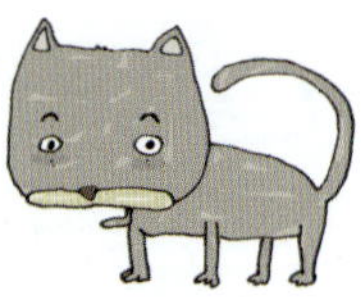 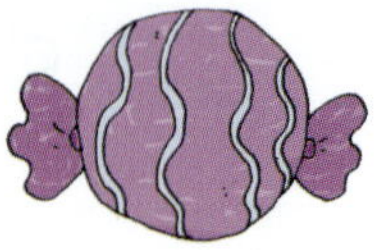 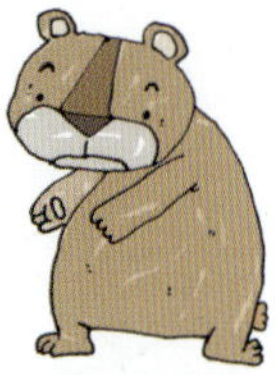

5. C c

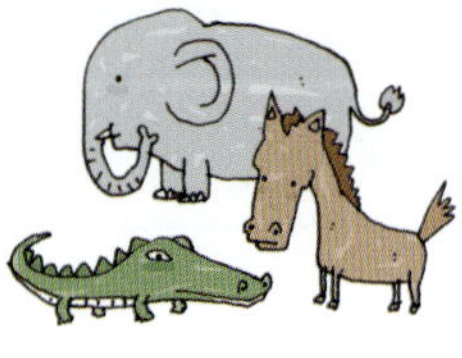 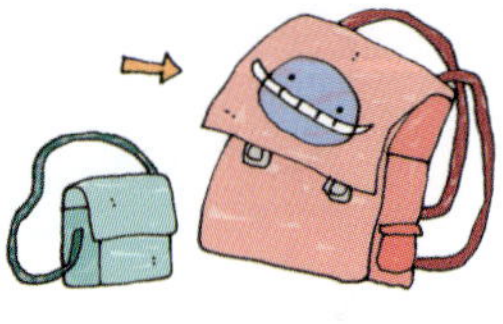 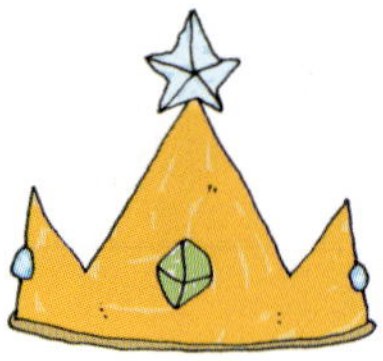

Circle and write the missing letter.

1
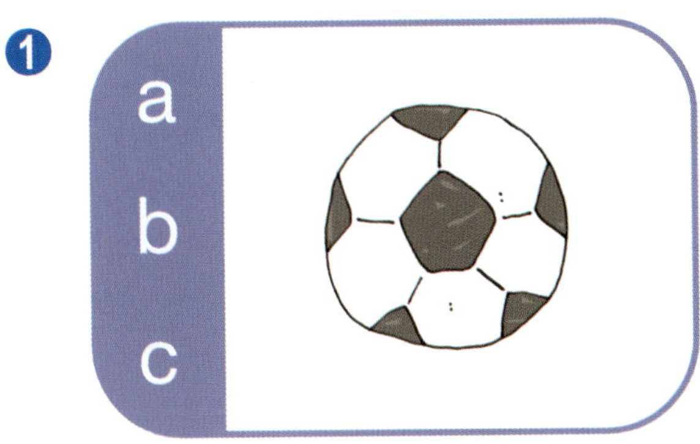

__ a l l

2

__ p p l e

3

__ a n d y

4

__ a t

5

__ n t

6

__ e a r

LETTER SEARCH

Complete the crossword puzzle.

1 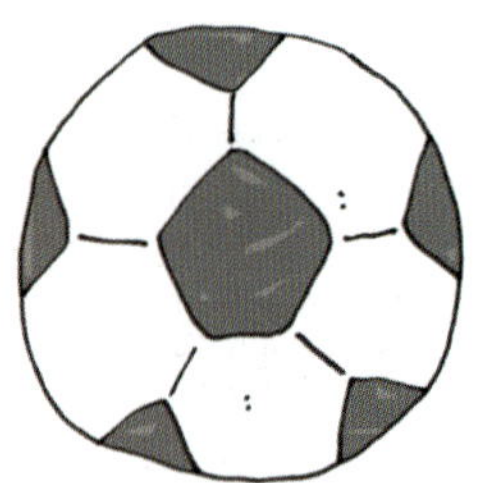

2 

3 

Crossword grid (with clue numbers 1., 5., 4.6., 2.3.):

5. e a r
l
4.6. p p l e
2.3. r o w n
a ... t
t

4 

5 

6 

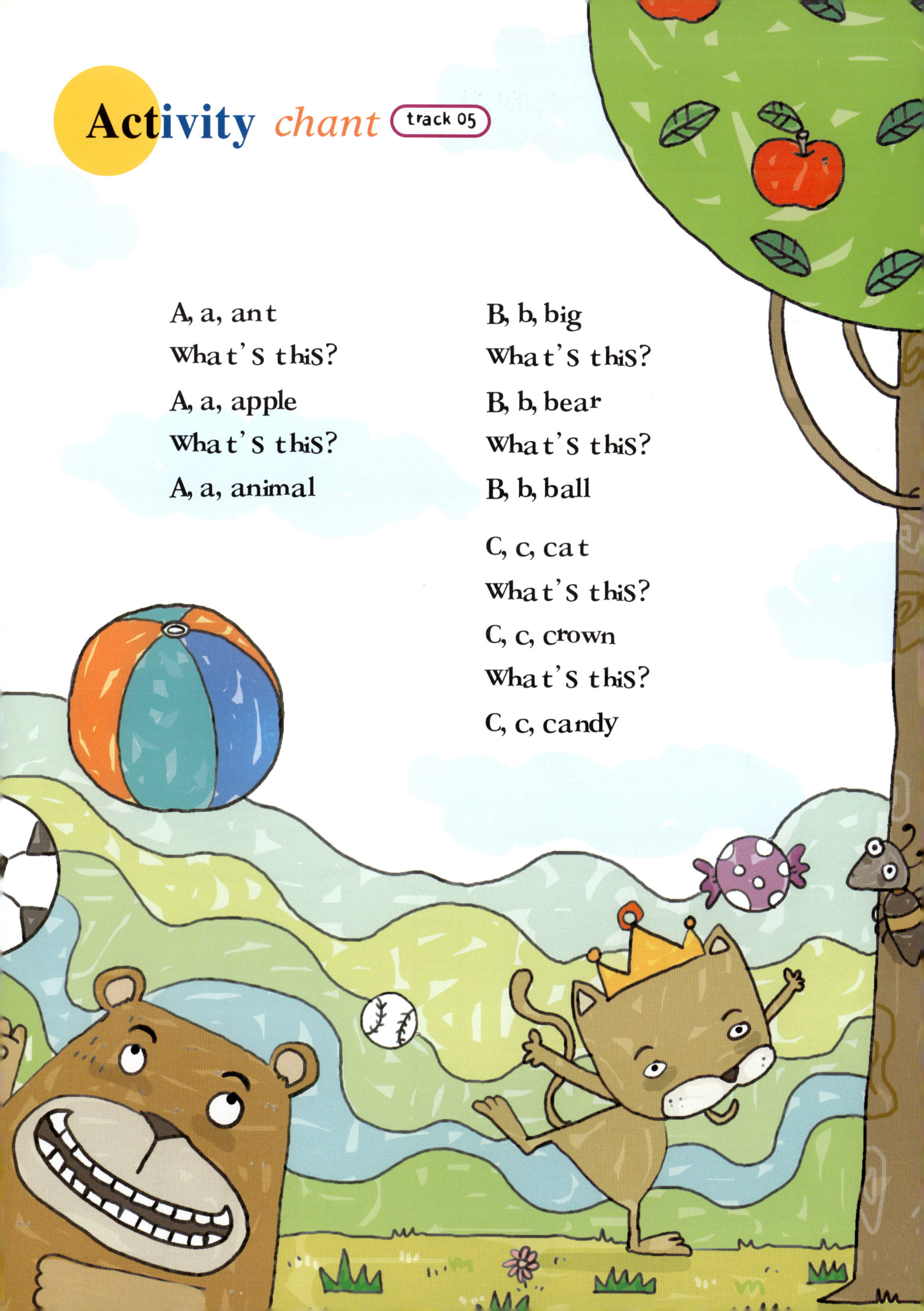

Activity *chant* track 05

A, a, ant
What's this?
A, a, apple
What's this?
A, a, animal

B, b, big
What's this?
B, b, bear
What's this?
B, b, ball

C, c, cat
What's this?
C, c, crown
What's this?
C, c, candy

Unit 2 Alphabet Dd Ee Ff
14
13

A **d**irty **d**og and a **d**uck
take the **e**levator.
An **E**skimo and
an **e**lephant
take the **e**levator.
A **f**ork and a **f**rog take the **e**levator.
Oh, the **e**levator is **f**ull.

Listen and repeat.

D d

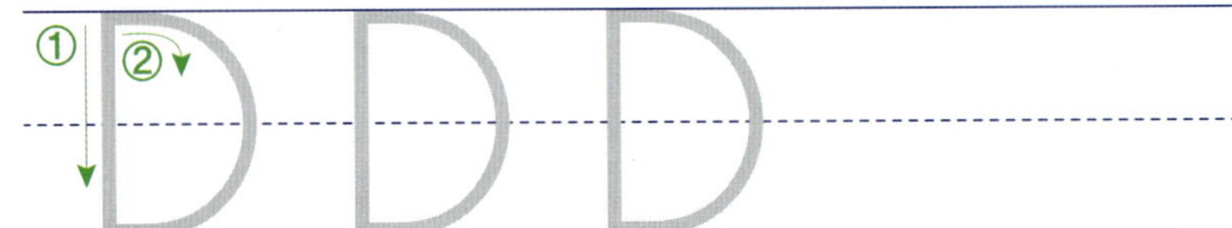

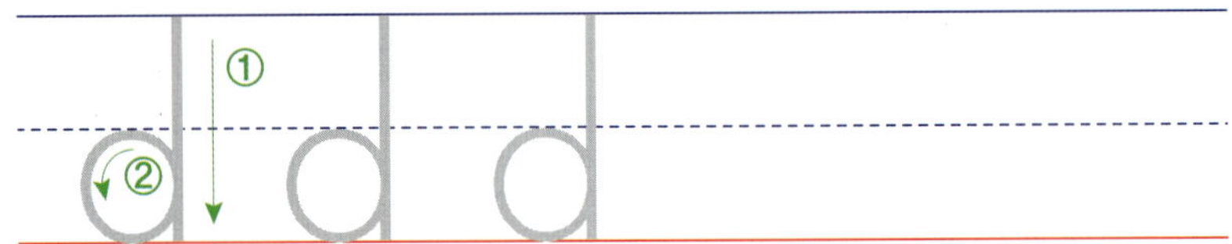

E e

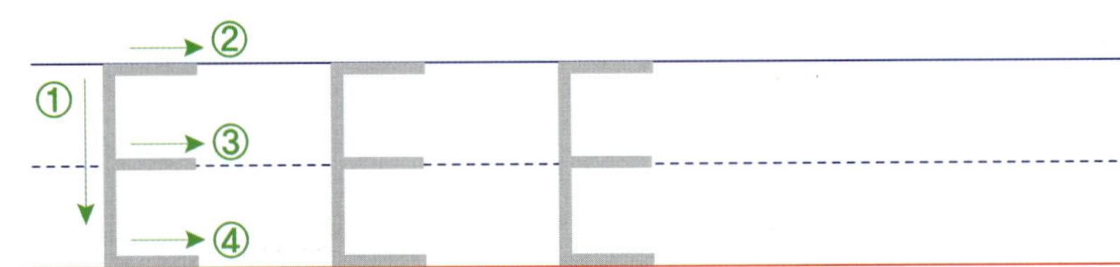

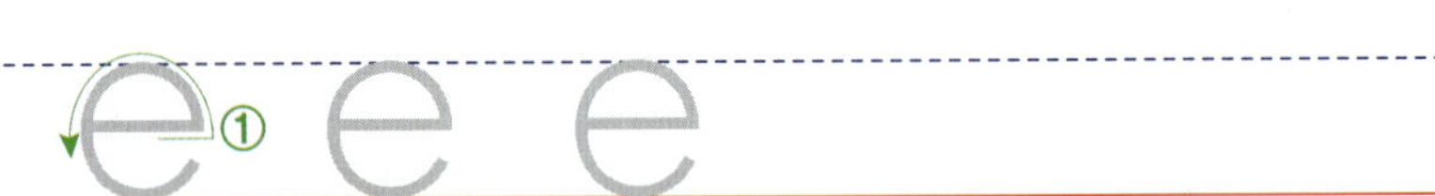

F f

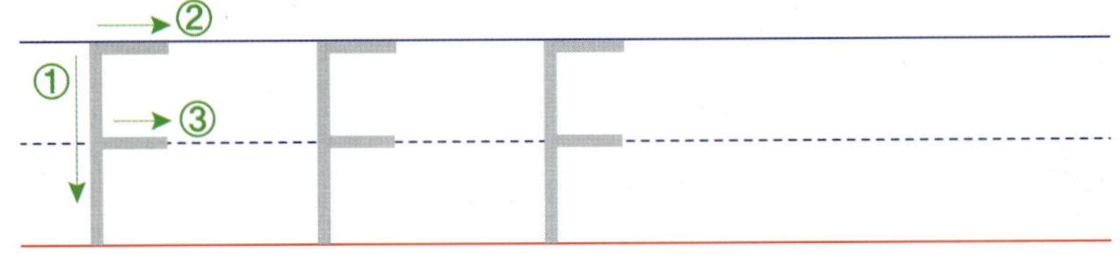

NEW WORDS

Listen, point and repeat. **track 08**

D
d

dirty

dog

duck

E
e

Eskimo

elephant

elevator

F
f

fork

frog

full

Listen to the beginning sound and circle `track 09` the correct picture.

1 

2 

3 

4 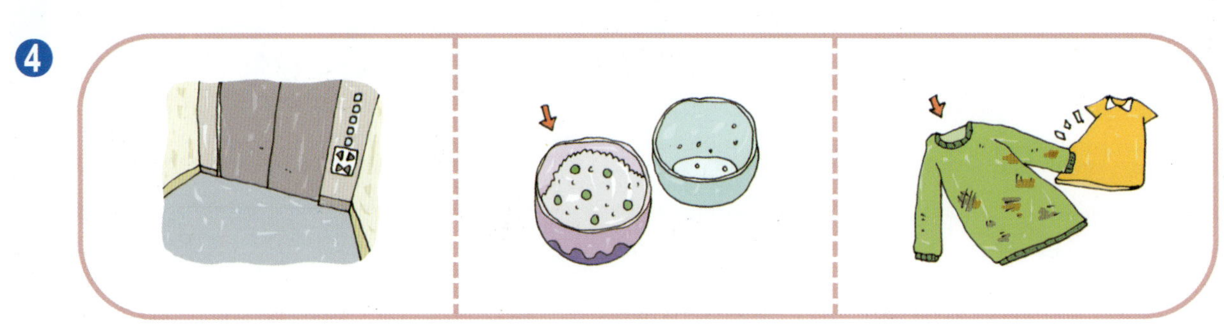

Color the same sound with the same color.

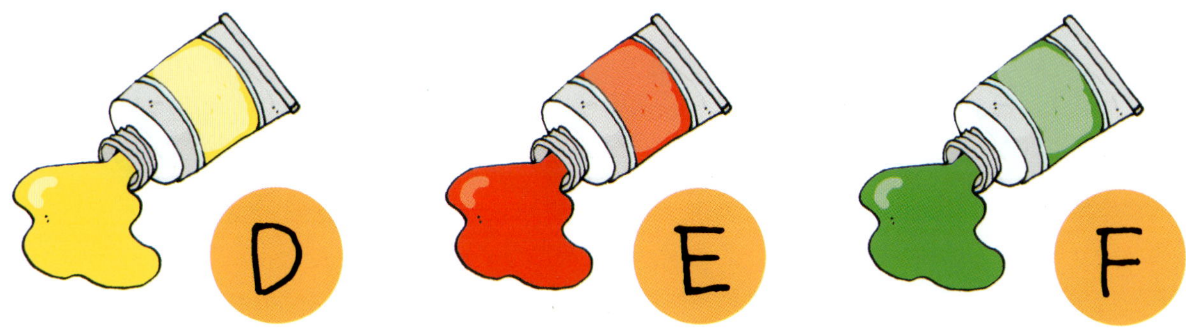

Match the letter with the picture.

1 F f • • 

2 E e • • 

3 D d • • 

4 E e • • 

5 F f • • 

Find and complete the word.

1. ___ u l l

2. ___ u c k

3. ___ s k i m o

4. ___ o g

5. ___ r o g

E   b   f   d   a   c

Complete the crossword puzzle.

Activity *chant* (track 10)

It's dirty.
D, d, duck.
D, d, dog.
It's a duck and a dog.

It's an Eskimo.
E, e, elephant.
E, e, elevator.
It's an elephant and an elevator.

It's full.
F, f, fork.
F, f, frog.
It's a fork and a frog.

Unit 3 Alphabet Gg Hh Ii

A **g**orilla plays the **g**uitar
in the **g**arden.
A **h**en and a **h**orse
play on the **h**ill.
An **I**ndian and
an **i**guana play with
the **i**nsect.

Listen and repeat. **track 12**

G g

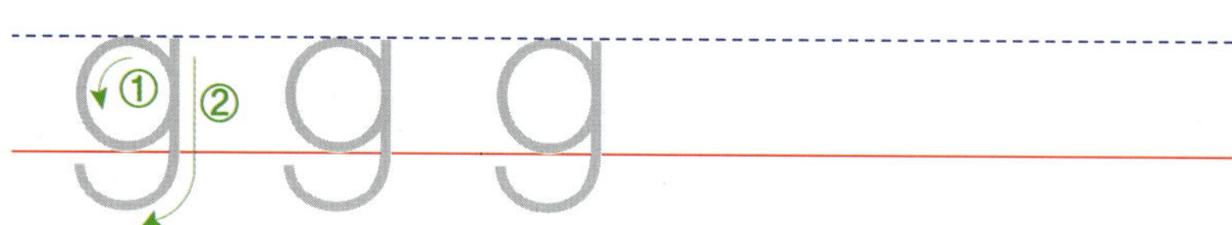

H h

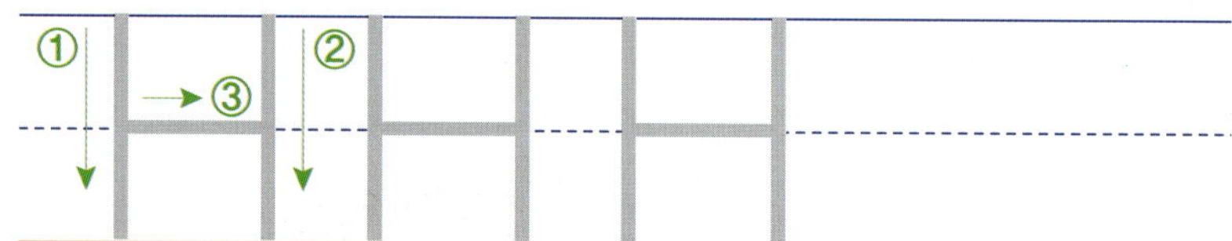

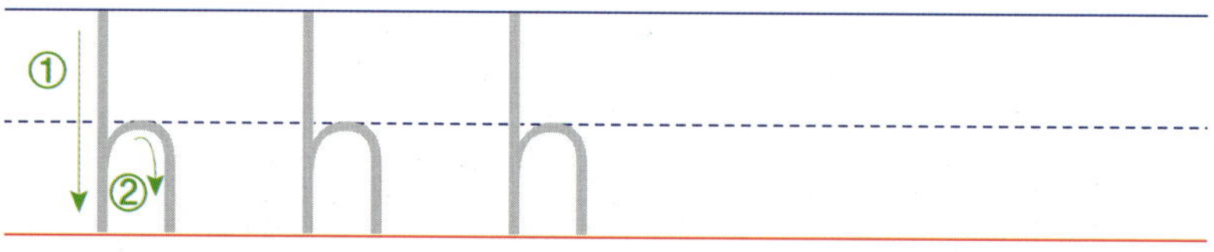

I i

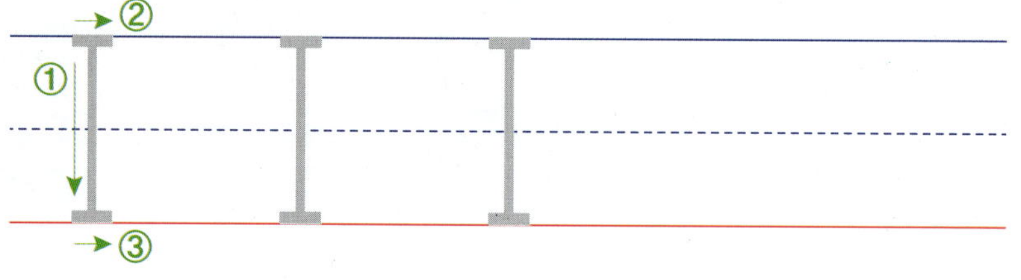

Listen, point and repeat. **track 13**

G
g

gorilla

guitar

garden

H
h

hen

horse

hill

I
i

Indian

iguana

insect

Listen to the word and write the beginning letter. track 14

① 

② 

③ 

④ 

⑤ 

⑥ 

⑦ 

⑧ 

⑨ 

Color the same sound with the same color.

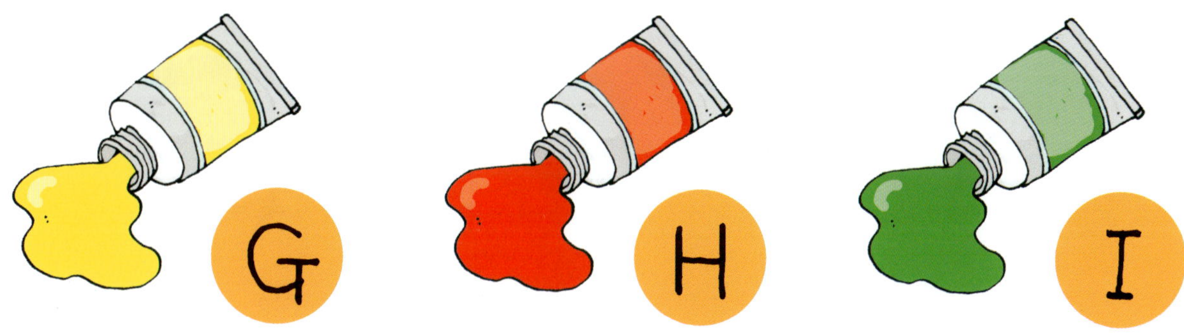

Look at the picture and circle the correct letter.

1

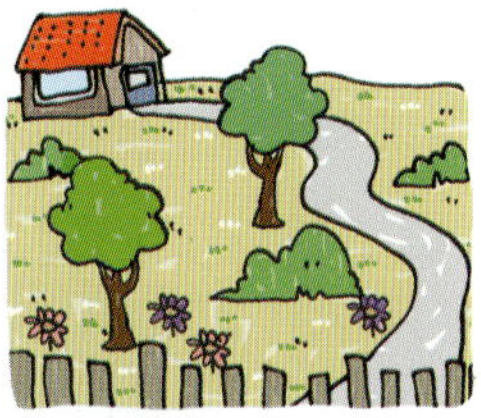

Gg   Hh

2

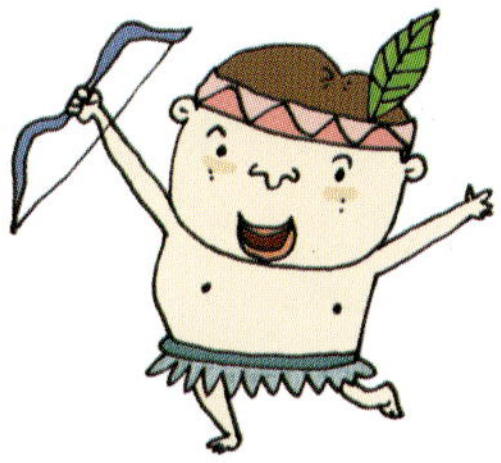

Ii   Gg

3

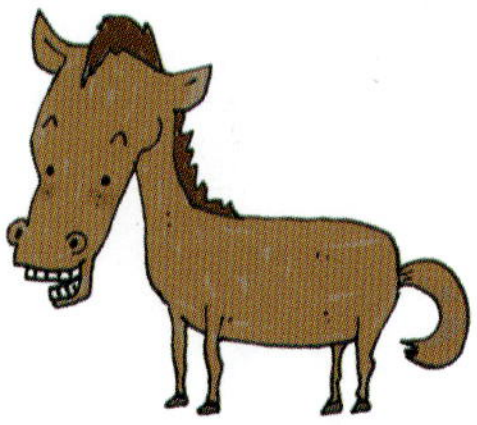

Ii   Hh

4

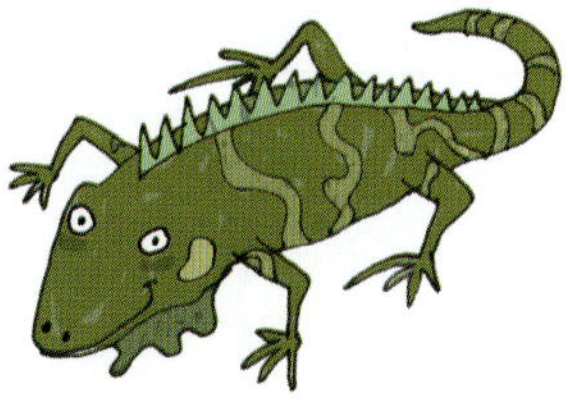

Gg   Ii

5

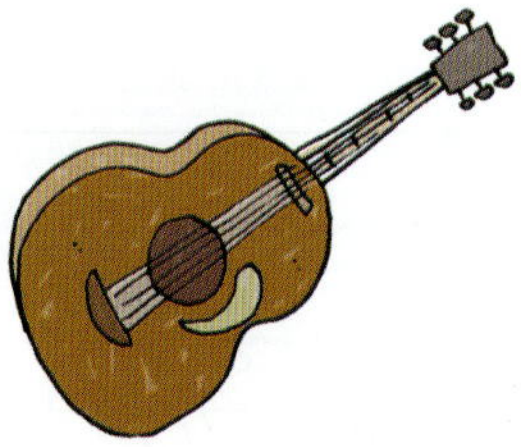

Hh   Gg

6

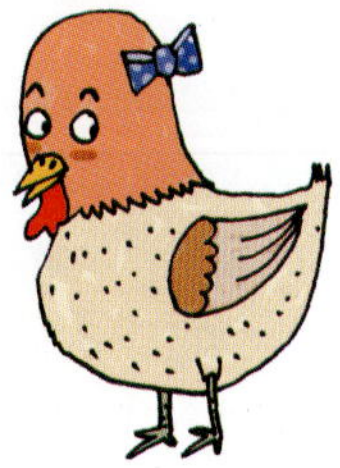

Hh   Ii

Circle and write the beginning letter for the picture.

1
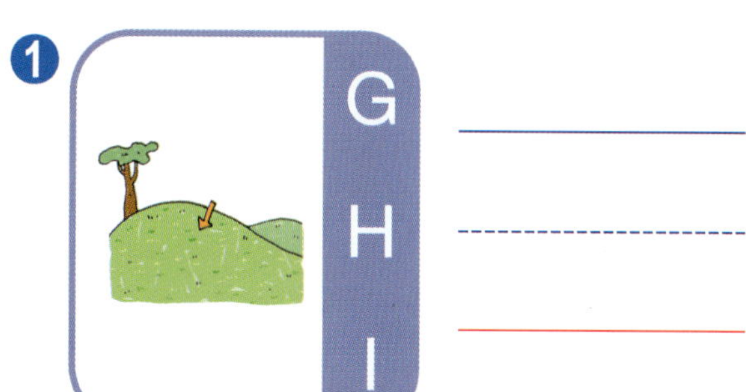

G
H
I

2

G
H
I

3

g
h
i

4

g
h
i

5

G
H
I

6

G
H
I

7

g
h
i

8

g
h
i

Complete the crossword puzzle.

1 

2 

3 

		1.							
		a		6.	u	2.	t	a	r
3.4.	o	r	s	e		g			
e		d				u			
n		e				a			
	5.	n	d	i	a	n			
						a			

4 

5 

6 

G, g, G, g, guitar.
Where is the gorilla?
The gorilla is in the garden.

H, h, H, h, horse.
Where is the hen?
The hen is on the hill.

I, i, I, i, insect.
Where is the Indian?
The Indian is by the iguana.

Listen to the word and circle the correct picture. track 16

1 

2 

3 

4 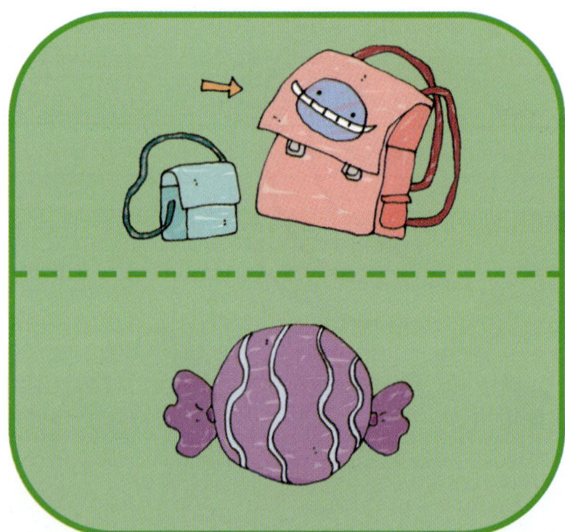

5 

6 

Circle the beginning letters.

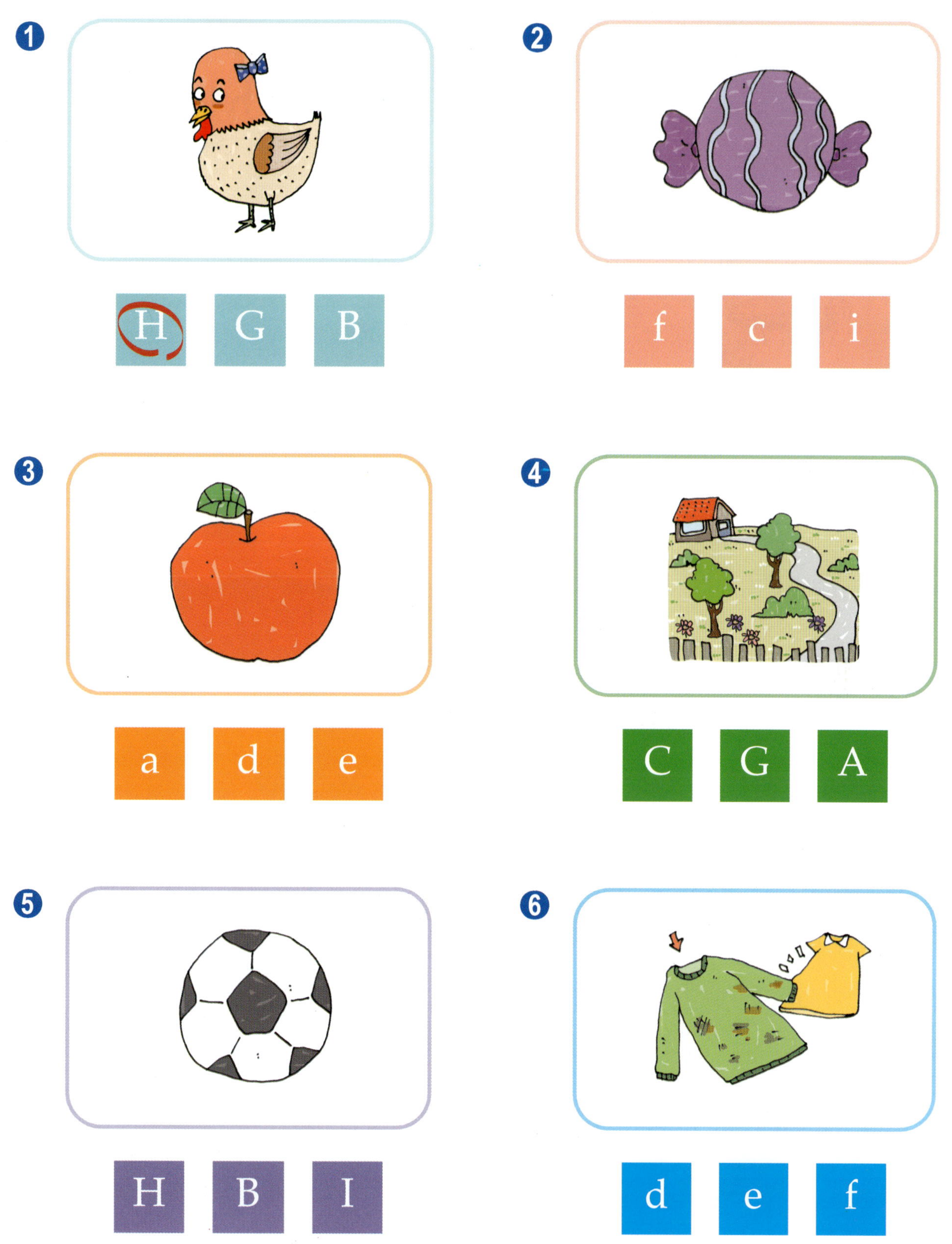

Find and circle the correct letters.

1.

B I C F d h e i

2.

A E D G c i f b

3.

I F H C b a d e

4.

C G A F d b e h

5.

I H G E b c f a

Find and write the letter.

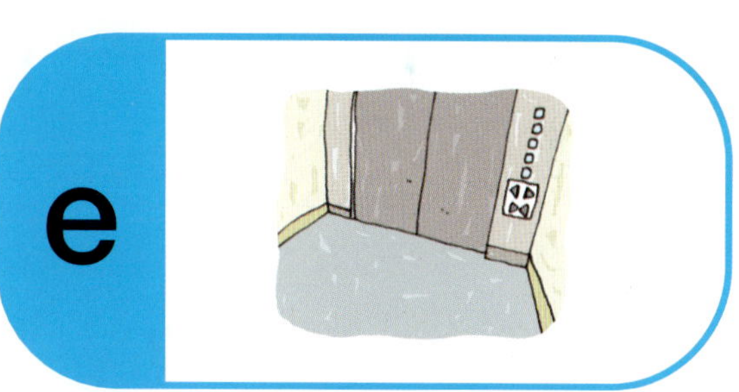

1 [c] at

2 [ ] irty

3 [ ] uitar

4 [ ] ill

5 [ ] levator

6 [ ] nt

Unit 4 Alphabet Jj Kk Ll

A jeep is in the jungle.
There is jam in the jeep.
A kangaroo kicks the kettle
in the jungle.
A lion has a lamp and a log
in the jungle.

Listen and repeat. track 18

J j

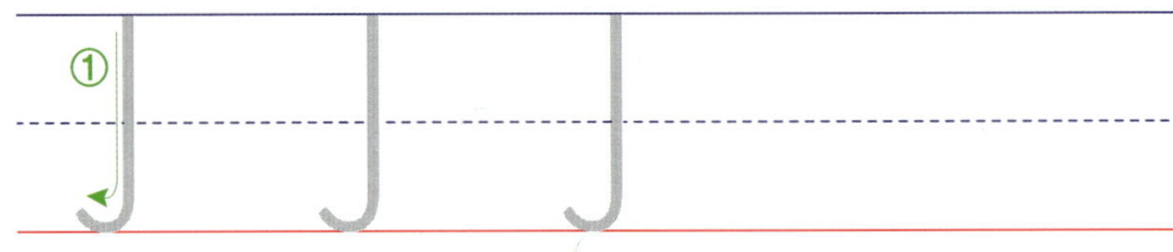

K k

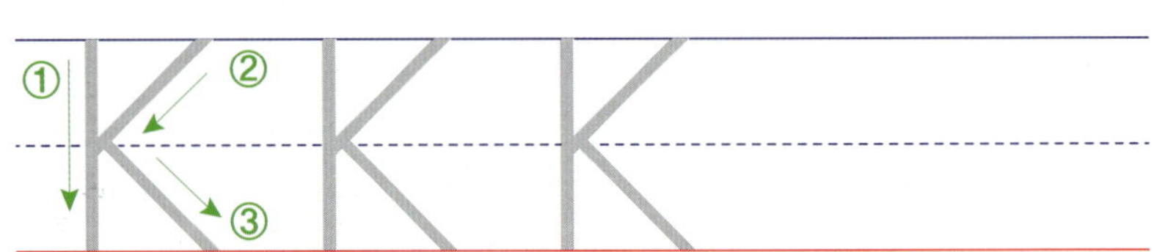

L l

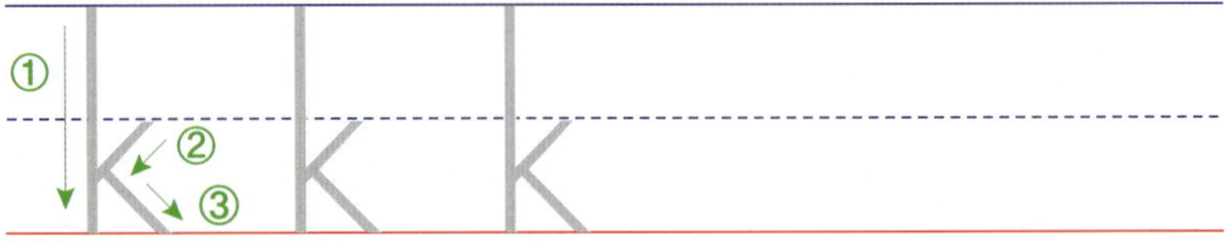

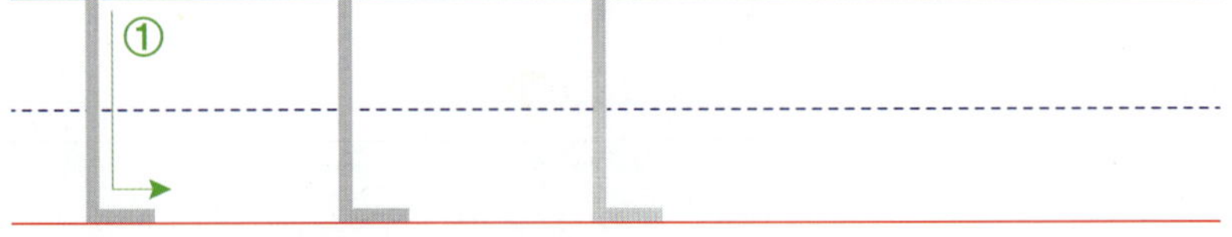

Listen, point and repeat. track 19 

J

j

jeep

jungle

jam

K

k

kangaroo

kick

kettle

L

l

lion

lamp

log

PRACTICE - LISTEN

Listen and check the beginning sound letter.   track 20

1

j   k   l

2

j   k   l

3

j   k   l

4

j   k   l

5

j   k   l

6

j   k   l

Color the same sound with the same color.

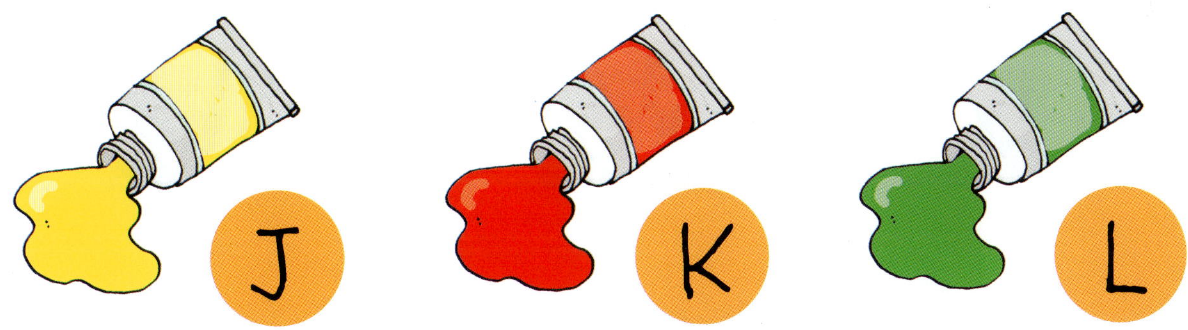

PRACTICE - READ

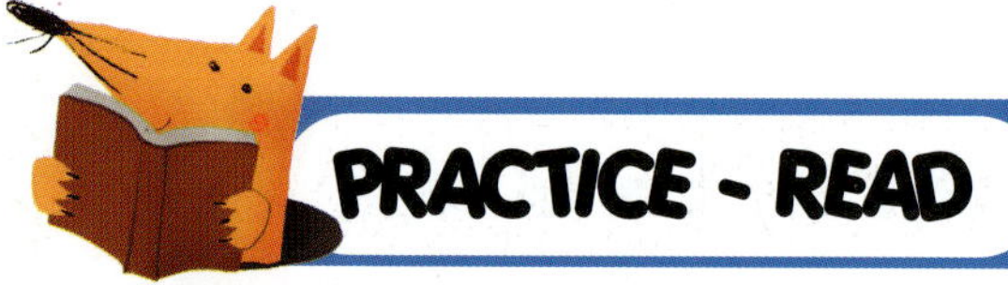

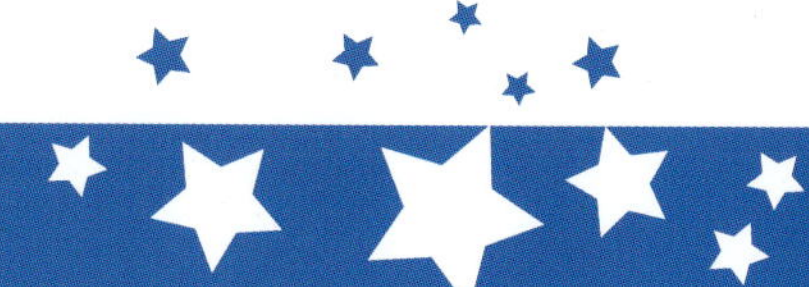

Read and circle the correct picture.

1. L l

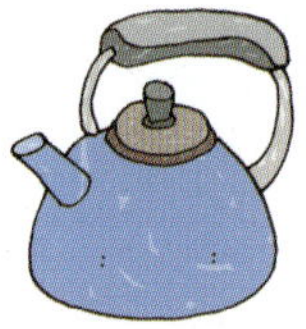 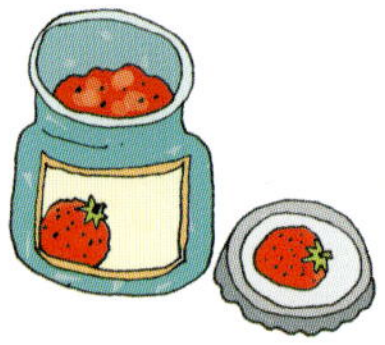 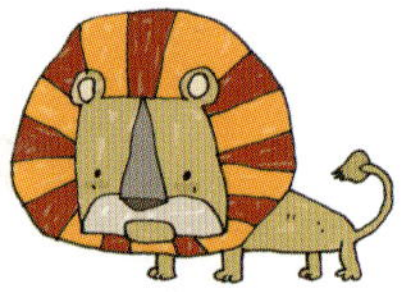

2. J j

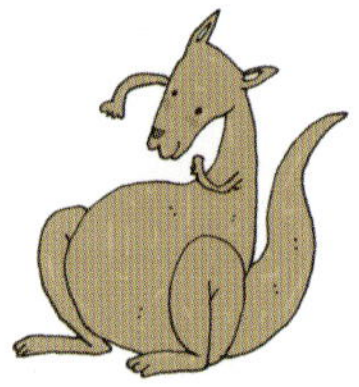 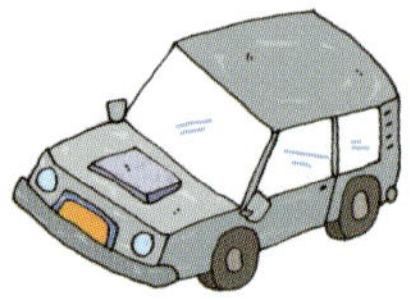 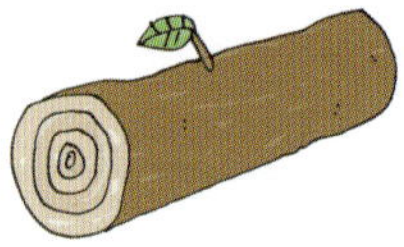

3. K k

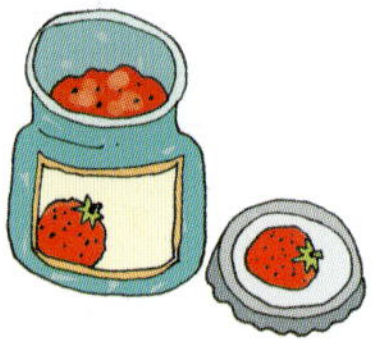 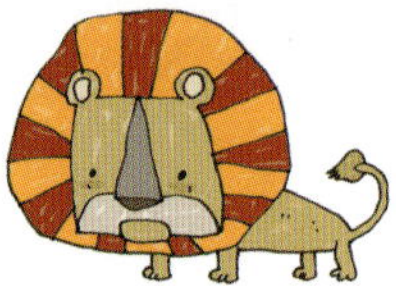 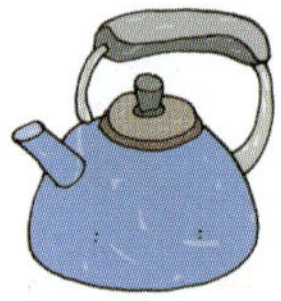

4. J j

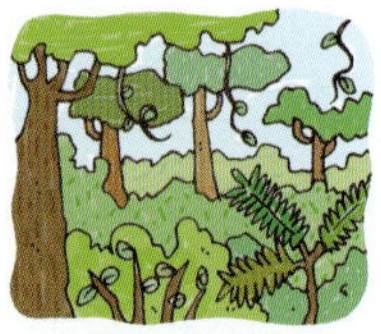 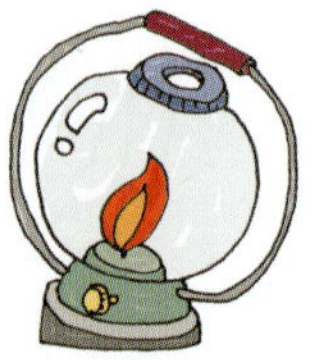 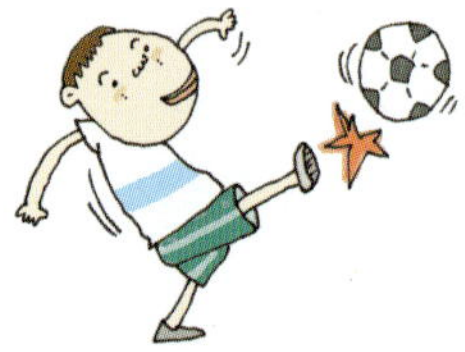

5. L l

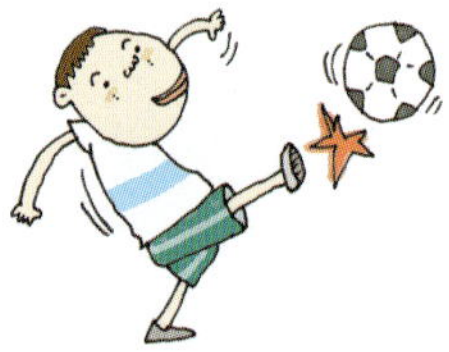 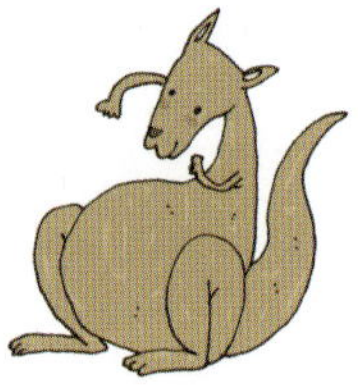 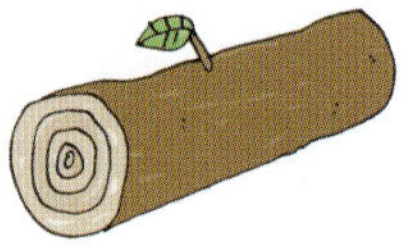

Circle and write the missing letter.

1

j
k
l

__ a m

2

j
k
l

__ e t t l e

3

j
k
l

__ o g

4

j
k
l

__ i c k

5

j
k
l

__ e e p

6

j
k
l

__ i o n

LETTER SEARCH

Complete the crossword puzzle.

1

2

3

1.									
i		4.				5.6.	a	m	p
c		u				i			
2.	a	n	g	a	r	o	o		
		g				n			
		l							
	3.	e	e	p					

4

5

6

J, j, J, j, jungle
I have jam.
J, j, J, j, jam.
I have a jeep.
J, j, J, j, jeep.

K, k, K, k, kick
I have a kangaroo.
K, k, K, k, kangaroo
I have a kettle.
K, k, K, k, kettle

L, l, L, l, lion
I have a lamp.
L, l, L, l, lamp
I have a log.
L, l, L, l, log

A monkey makes a mask.
Nine nuts make a net.
An octopus makes an omelet
with an ostrich.

Listen and repeat. **track 23**

M m

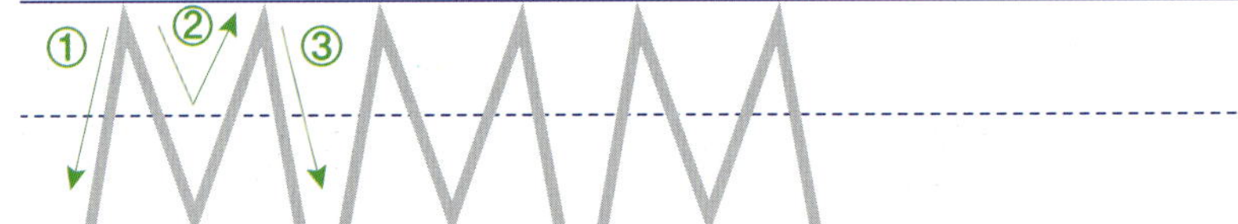

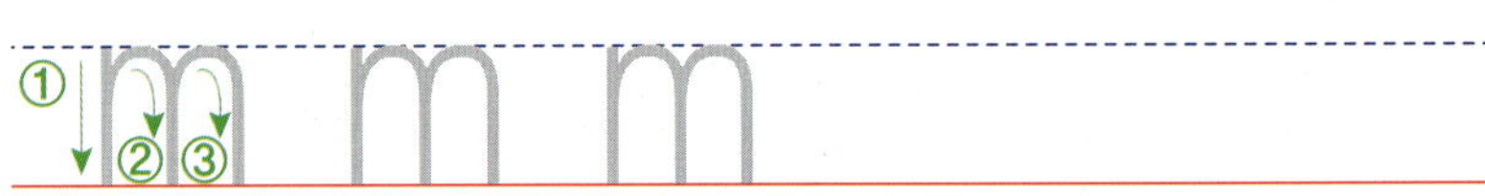

N n

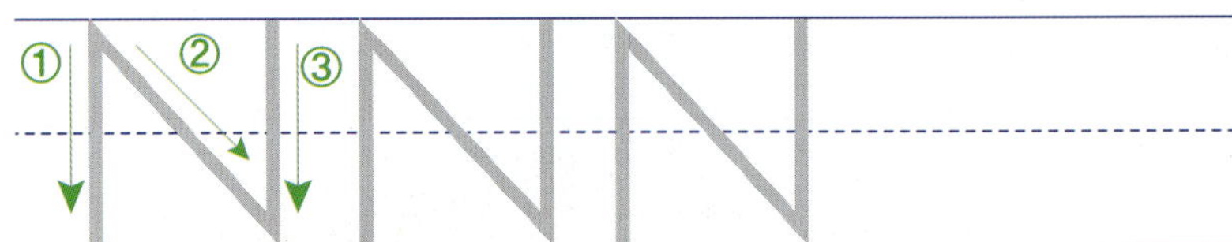

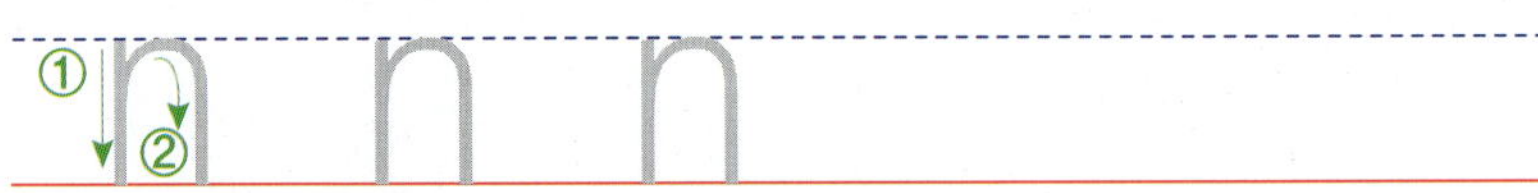

O o

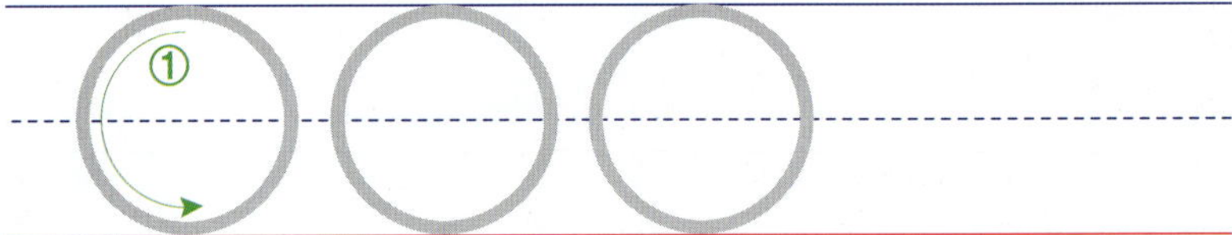

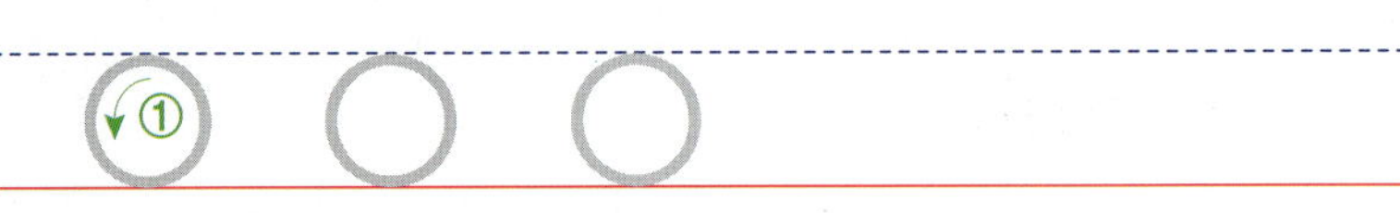

Listen, point and repeat. **track 24**

M
m

monkey

make

mask

N
n

nine

nut

net

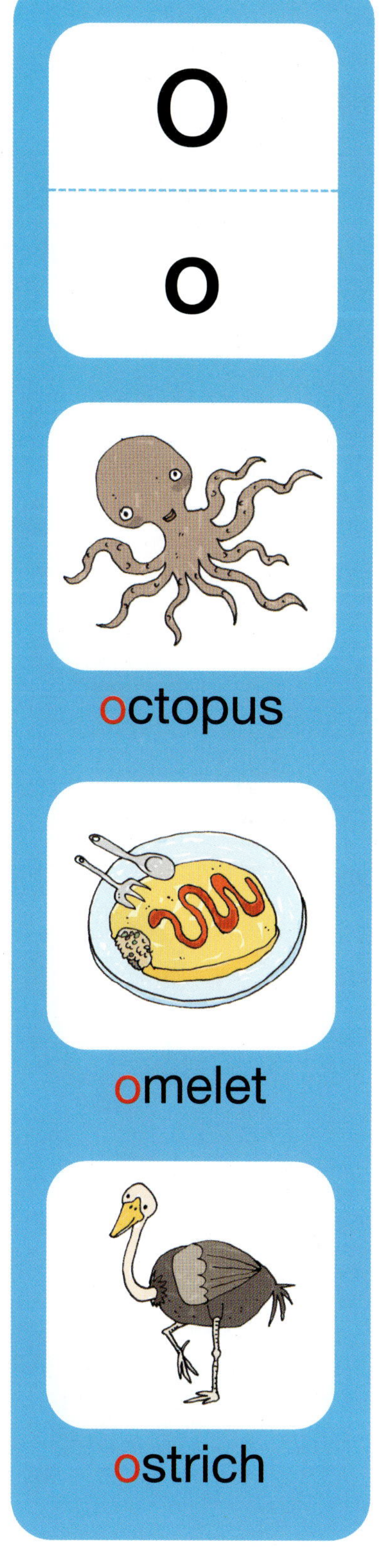

O
o

octopus

omelet

ostrich

Listen to the beginning sound and circle (track 25) the correct picture.

1

2

3

4

Color the same sound with the same color.

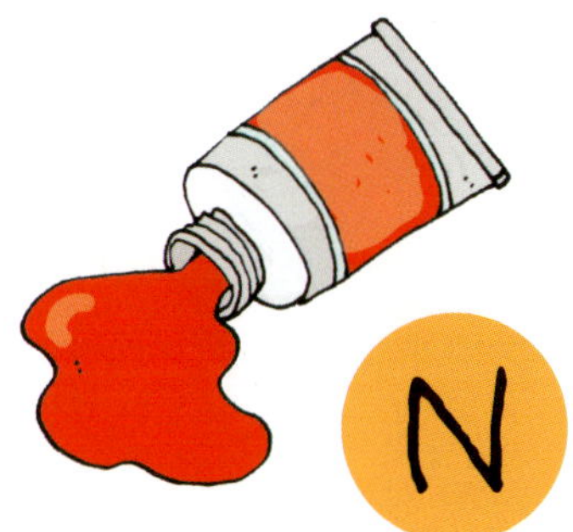

M

N

O

Match the letter with the picture.

① N n

② O o

③ M m

④ N n

⑤ O o

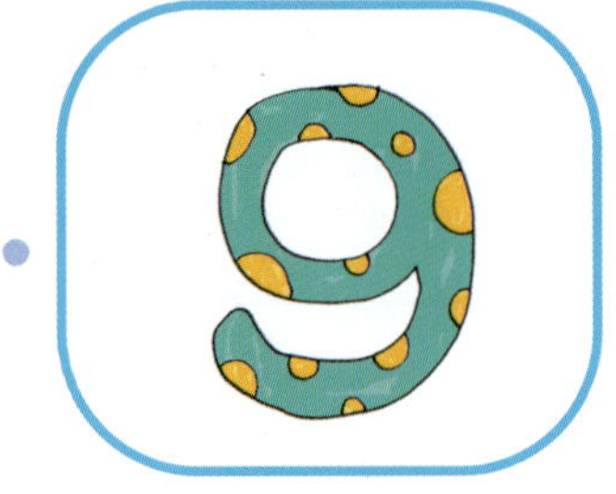

Find and complete the word.

1.  ☐ m e l e t

2.  ☐ a s k

3.  ☐ e t

4. 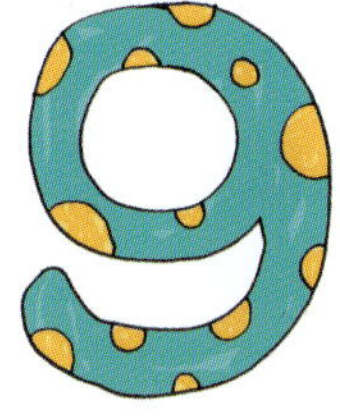 ☐ i n e

5.  ☐ a k e

l   n   i   o   k   m   h

Complete the crossword puzzle.

1
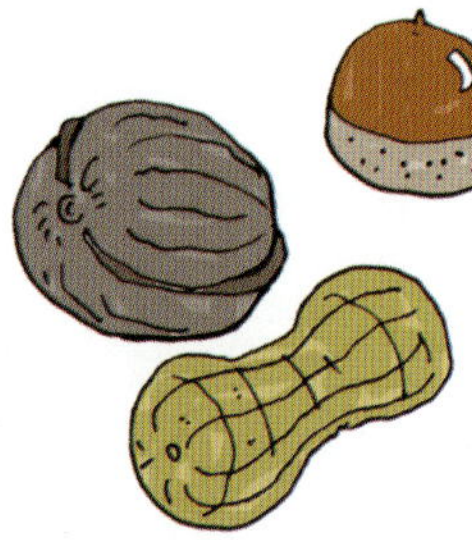

2
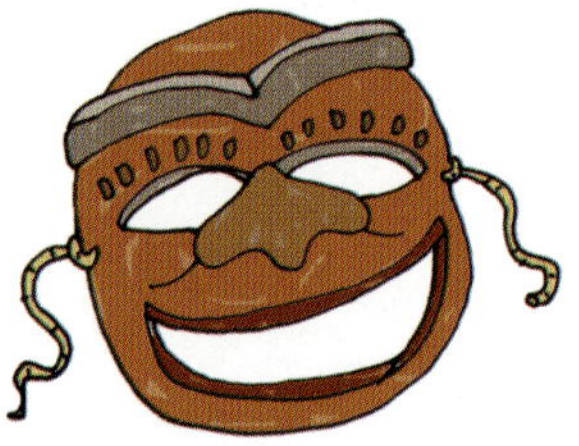

3
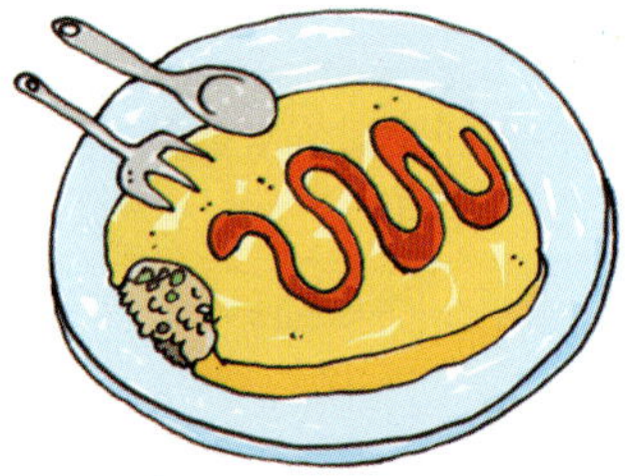

		1.				2.4.	a	k	e
		u				a			
5.	c	t	3.	p	u	s			
			m			k			
			e						
			l						
			e						
	6.	e	t						

4
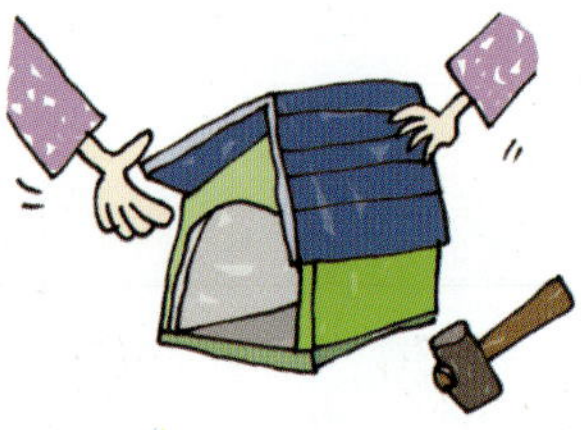

5
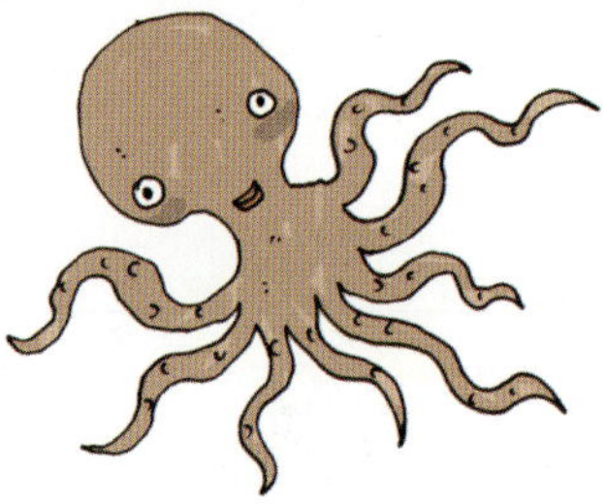

6
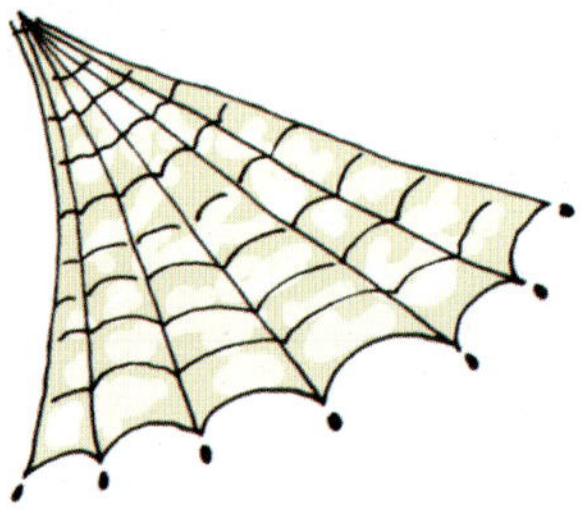

M, m, M, m make!
Who am I?
I have a maSk.
Monkey, monkey, monkey.

N, n, N, n nine!
Who am I?
I have a net.
Nut, nut, nut.

O, o, O, o oStrich!
Who am I?
I have an omelet.
OctopuS, octopuS, octopuS.

Unit 6 Alphabet Pp Qq Rr

track 27
A pink pig paints a rocket.
A quail paints a queen
and a quilt.
A rabbit paints a rose.

Listen and repeat. **track 28**

P p

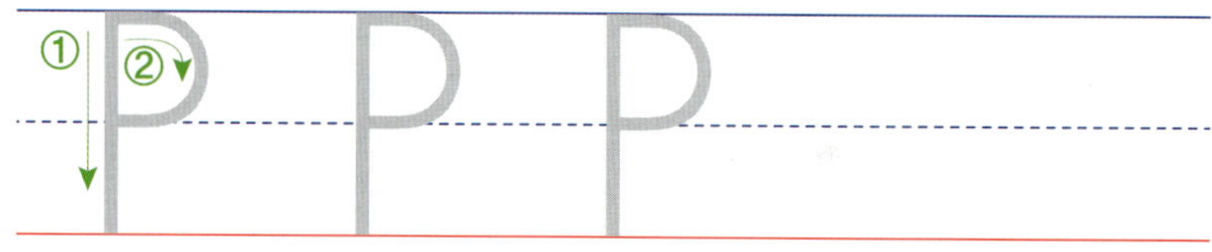

Q q

R r

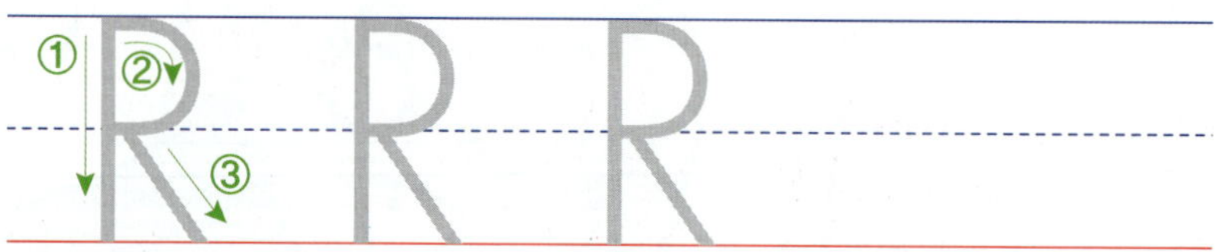

Listen, point and repeat. **track 29**

Listen to the word and write the beginning letter. 

 1 

2 

3 

4 

5 

6 

7 

8 

9 

Color the same sound with the same color.

Look at the picture and circle the correct letter.

1

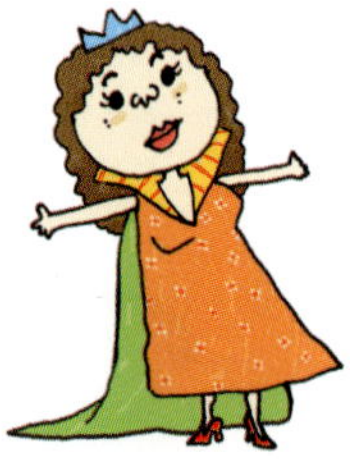

Qq | Rr

2

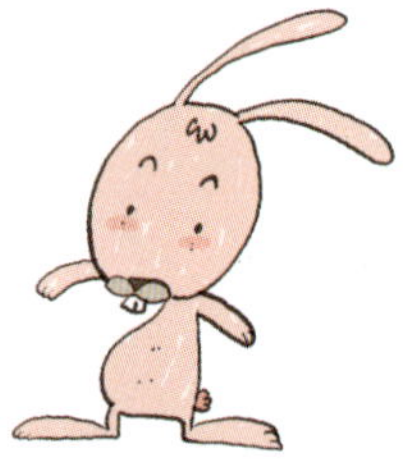

Rr | Pp

3

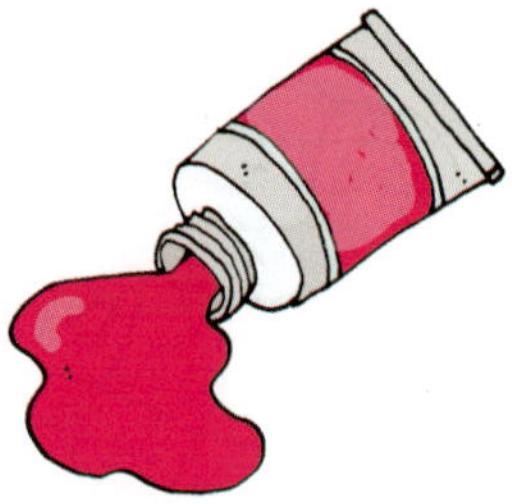

Pp | Qq

4

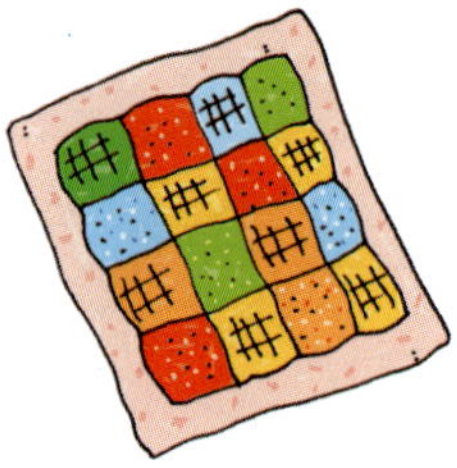

Rr | Qq

5

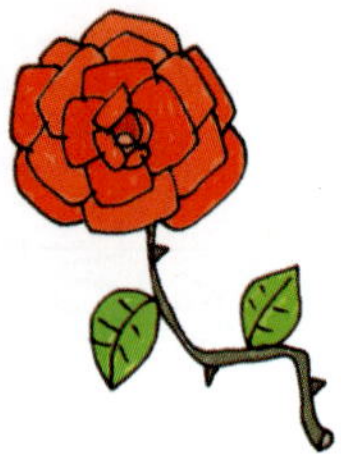

Rr | Pp

6

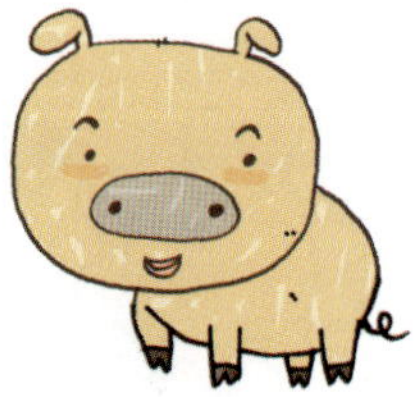

Qq | Pp

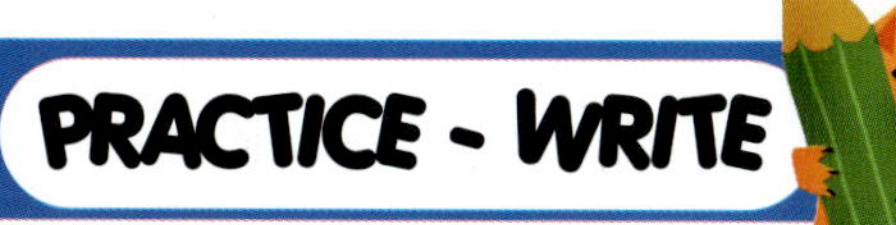

Circle and write the beginning letter for the picture.

1 

P
Q
R

2 

P
Q
R

3 

p
q
r

4 

p
q
r

5 

P
Q
R

6 

P
Q
R

7 

p
q
r

8 

p
q
r

LETTER SEARCH

Complete the crossword puzzle.

1

2

3

							3.		
							o		5.
							s		i
					4.6.	u	e	e	n
					u				k
			2.	a	i	n	t		
					l				
1.	o	c	k	e	t				

4

5

6

Activity *chant*  `track 31`

P, p, P, p, pink.
P, p, P, p, pig.
Look! A pink pig!
Not paint!

Q, q, Q, q, quail.
Q, q, Q, q, quilt.
Look! A quail on the quilt!
Not on the queen!

R, r, R, r, rabbit.
R, r, R, r, rocket.
Look! A rabbit in the rocket!
Not in the roses!

Listen to the word and circle the correct picture. track 32

1

2

3

4

5

6

Circle the beginning letters.

1. o m k r

2. l p n o

3. J M R L

4. k j q n

5. Q N P K

6. N L J R

REVIEW 2

Match and write the small letter.

1 M
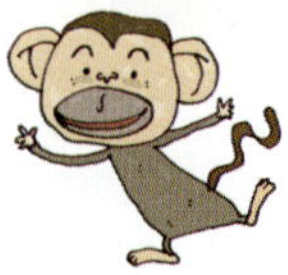

2 Q
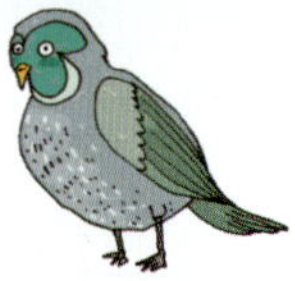

3 K
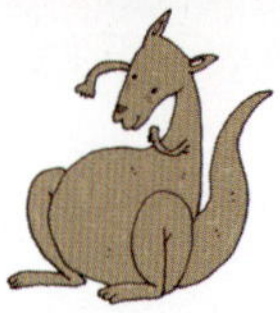

4 O
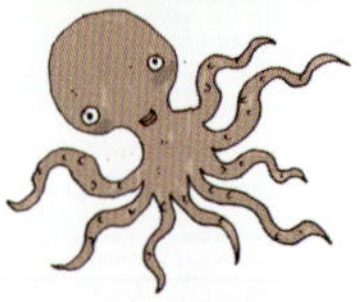

5 J
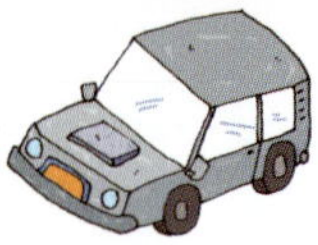

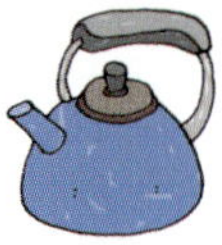

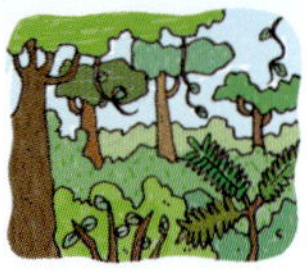

m
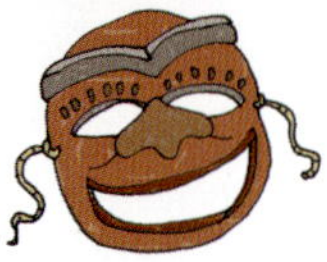

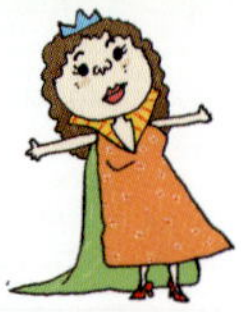

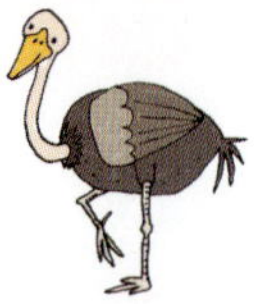

Find and write the beginning letter for the picture.

log   kettle   nine   omelet

queen   lion   rose   pink

Unit 7 Alphabet Ss Tt Uu

A **s**eal **s**ings in the **s**ea.
Twin **t**igers **s**ing between the **t**rees.
An **u**gly **u**ncle **s**ings
with an **u**mbrella.

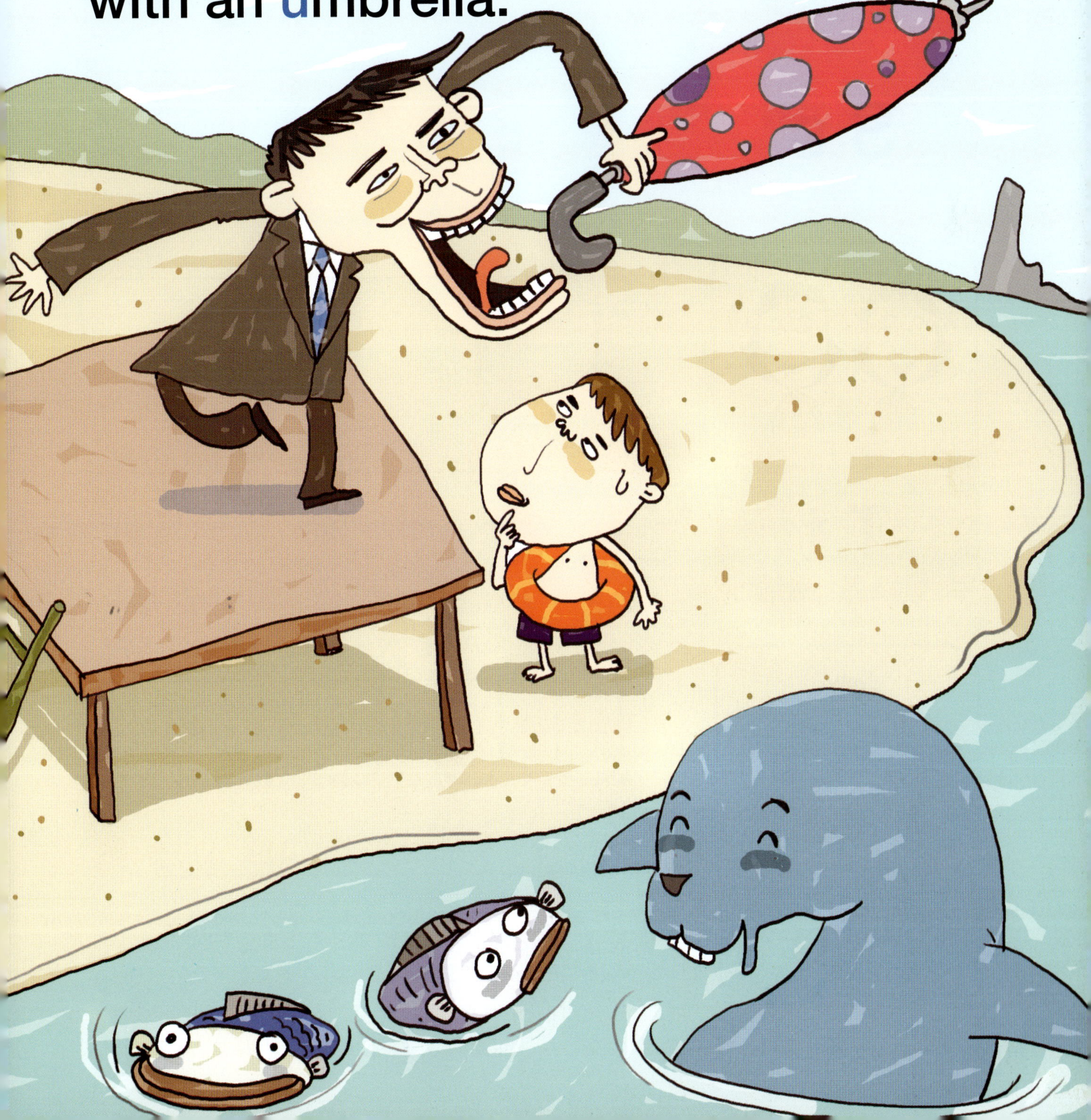

Listen and repeat. **track 34**

S s

T t

U u

Listen, point and repeat. **track 35**

S s

seal

sing

sea

T t

twins

tiger

tree

U u

ugly

uncle

umbrella

Listen and check the beginning sound letter. track 36

1 

s t u

2 

s t u

3 

s t u

4 

s t u

5 

s t u

6 

s t u

Color the same sound with the same color.

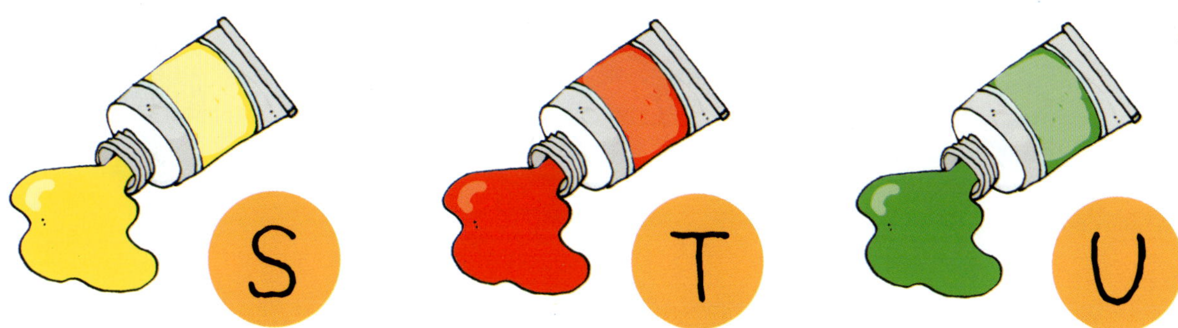

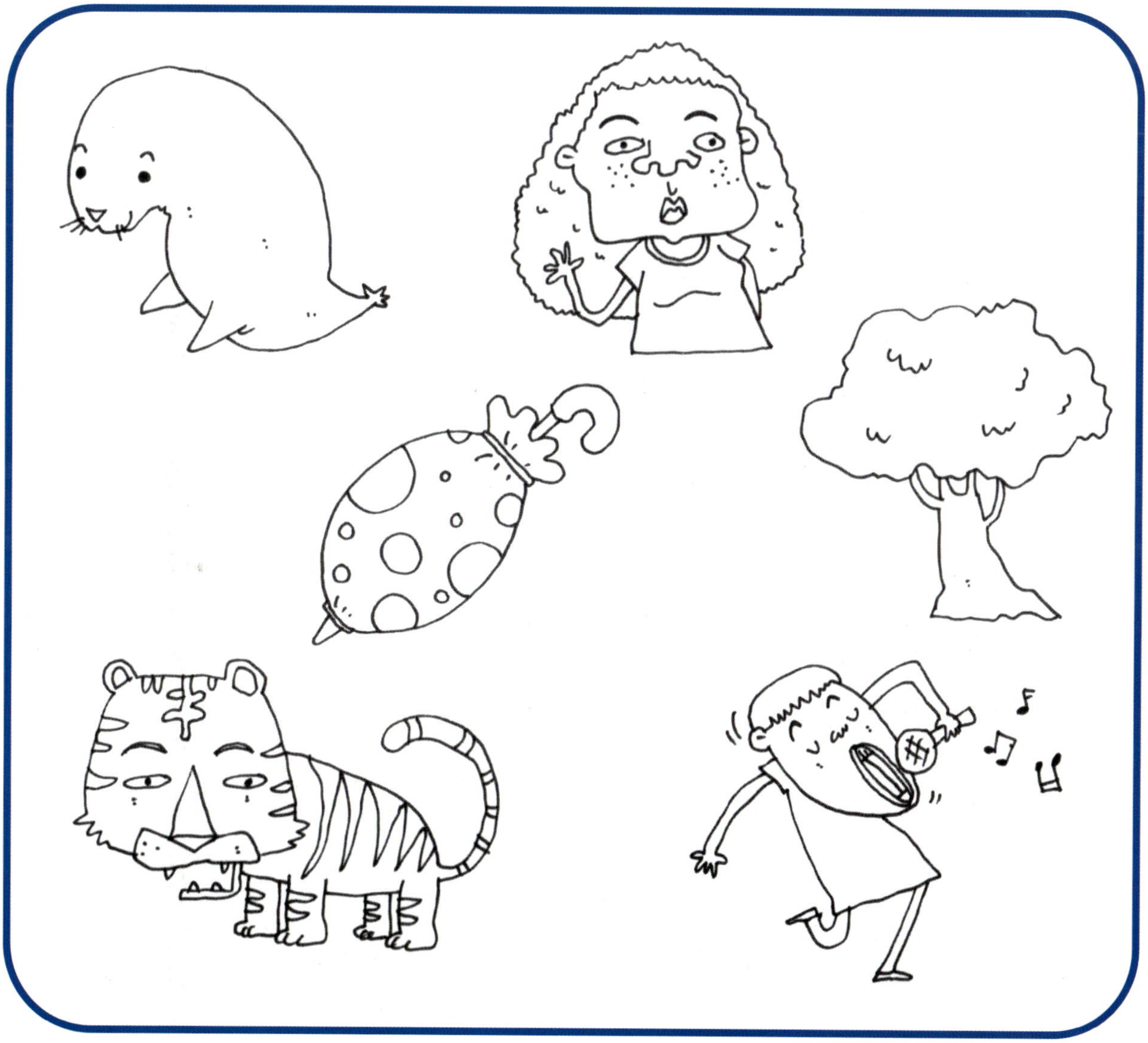

Read and circle the correct picture.

1 S s   

2 T t   

3 T t   

4 U u   

5 S s    

Circle and write the missing letter.

1

s
t
u

__ i g e r

2

s
t
u

__ m b r e l l a

3

s
t
u

__ e a

4

s
t
u

__ i n g

5

s
t
u

__ g l y

6

s
t
u

__ r e e

Complete the crossword puzzle.

Activity *chant* (track 37)

S, S, Sing.
What's your name?
I'm a S, S, Seal.
What's your name?
I'm a S, S, Sea.

T, t, twin.
What's your name?
I'm a T, t, tiger.
What's your name?
I'm a T, t, tree.

U, u, ugly.
What's your name?
I'm an U, u, uncle.
What's your name?
I'm an U, u, umbrella.

Unit 8 Alphabet Vv Ww Xx

A **v**ulture has a **v**ane.
A **w**olf has a **w**et **w**ig
and a **v**est.
Si**x** fo**x**es have the bo**x**.

Listen and repeat. track 39

V v

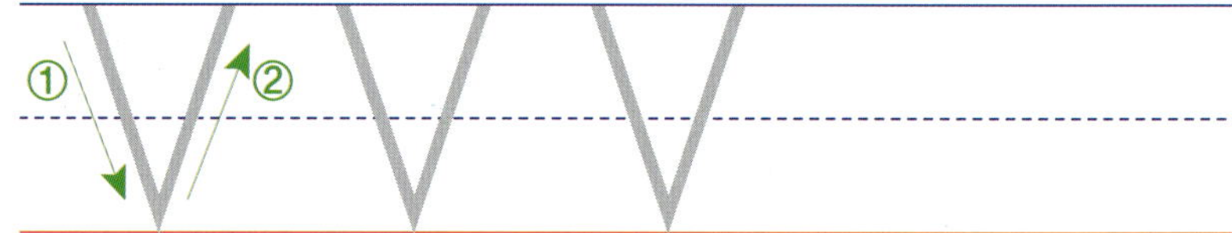

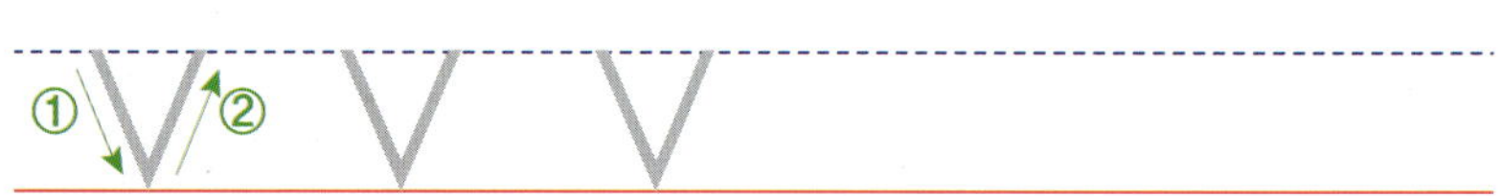

W w

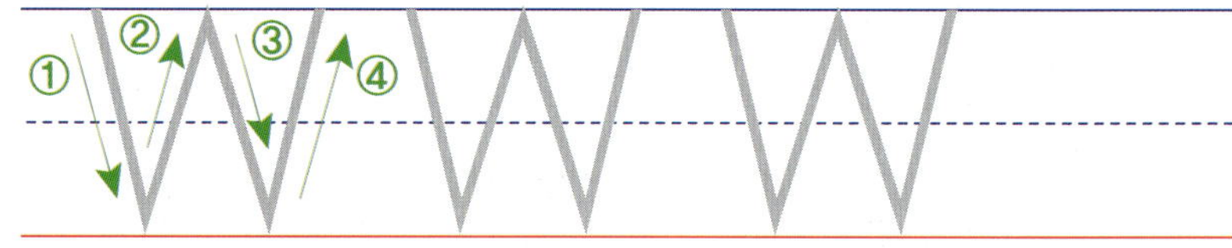

X x

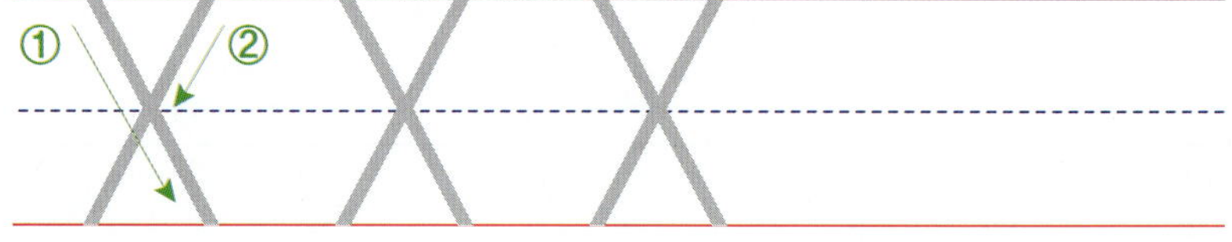

NEW WORDS

Listen, point and repeat. **track 40**

V
v

vulture

vane

vest

W
w

wolf

wet

wig

X
x

six

fox

box

Listen to the beginning(ending) sound and circle `track 41` the correct picture.

1 

2 

3 

4 

Color the same sound with the same color.

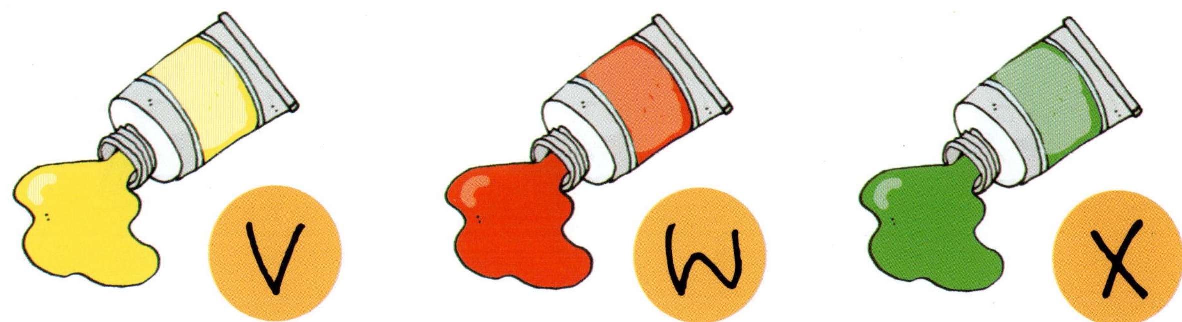

Match the letter with the picture.

① X x  ·   · 

② V v  ·   · 

③ W w  ·   · 

④ X x 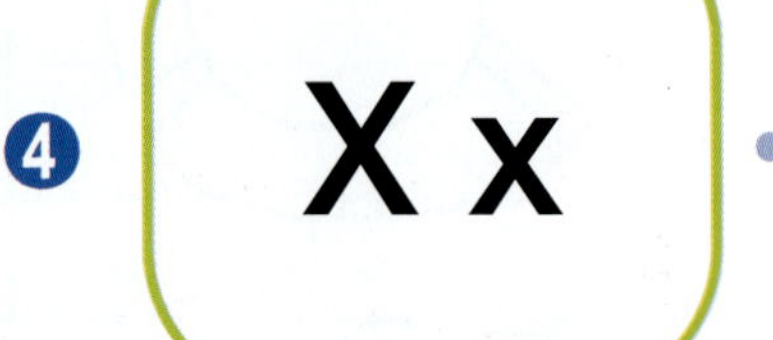 ·   · 

⑤ V v  ·   · 

Find and complete the word.

1.  | | e | s | t |

2.  | | o | l | f |

3.  | | e | t |

4.    f | o | |

5.  | a | n | e |

| s | x | t | v | u | w | r |

Complete the crossword puzzle.

1  **2**  **3** 

						5.		
1.	u	l	t	u	r	e		
						2. s	i	
				3.4.		e	t	
				o				
				l				
				6. f	o		.	

4  **5**  **6** 

Activity chant   track 42

V, v, vulture.
Where are you from?
I'm from a V, v, vane.
Where are you from?
I'm from a V, v, vest.

W, w, wet.
Where are you from?
I'm from a W, w, wolf.
Where are you from?
I'm from a W, w, wig.

X, x, six.
Where are you from?
I'm from a X, x, fox.
Where are you from?
I'm from a X, x, box.

ZOO

A yak yells in the zoo.
A zero and a zebra yawn
in the zoo.

Listen and repeat. 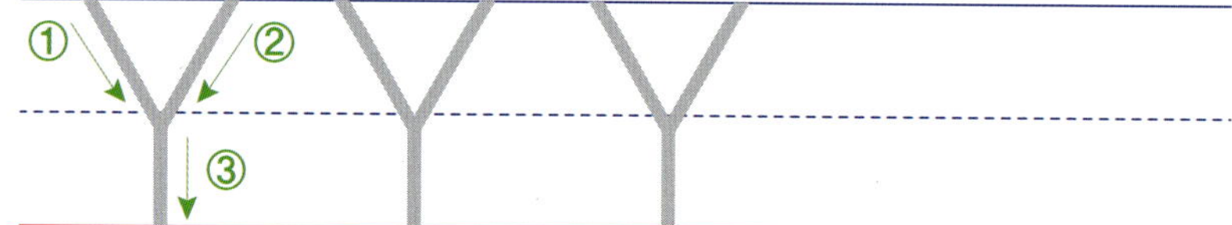 track 44

Y y

Z z

Listen, point and repeat. **track 45**

Y
y

yak

yell

yawn

Z
z

zoo

zero

zebra

Listen to the word and write the beginning letter.

 1

 2

 3

 4

 5

 6

Color the same sound with the same color.

Y

Z

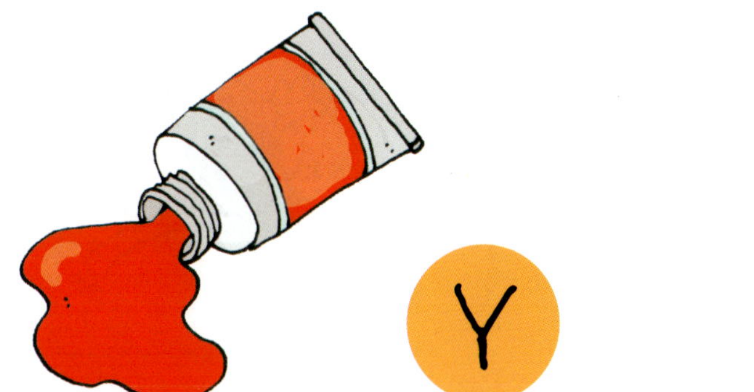

PRACTICE - READ

Look at the picture and chcek the correct letter.

1 Yy | Zz

2 Yy | Zz

3 Yy | Zz

4 Yy | Zz

5 Yy | Zz

6 Yy | Zz

Circle and write the beginning letter for the picture.

1

Y
Z

2

Y
Z

3

y
z

4

y
z

5

Y
Z

6

y
z

Complete the crossword puzzle.

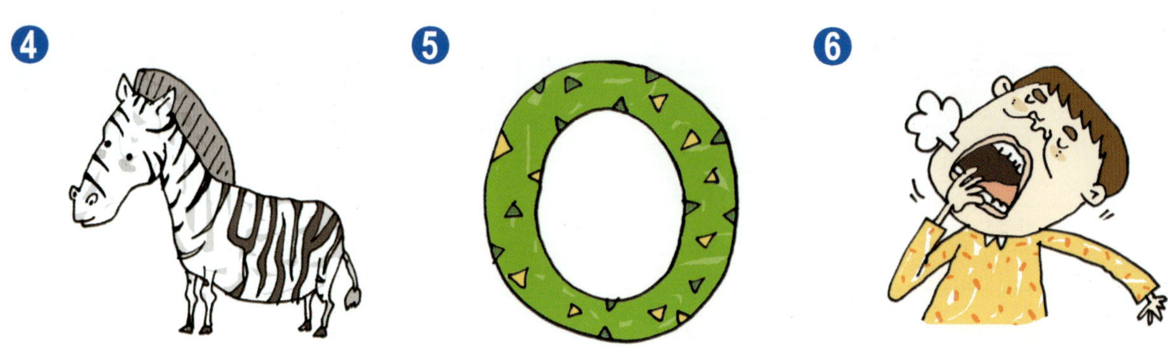

Activity *chant* track 47

Y, y, yell.
Y, y, yawn.
What do you have?
I have a Y, y, yak.

Z, z, zoo.
What do you have?
I have Z, z, zero.
What do you have?
I have a Z, z, zebra.

Listen and circle the right picture. track 48

Circle the right match.

1  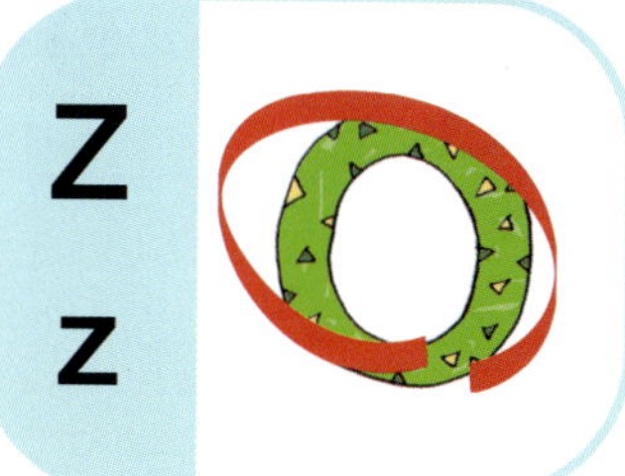 

2 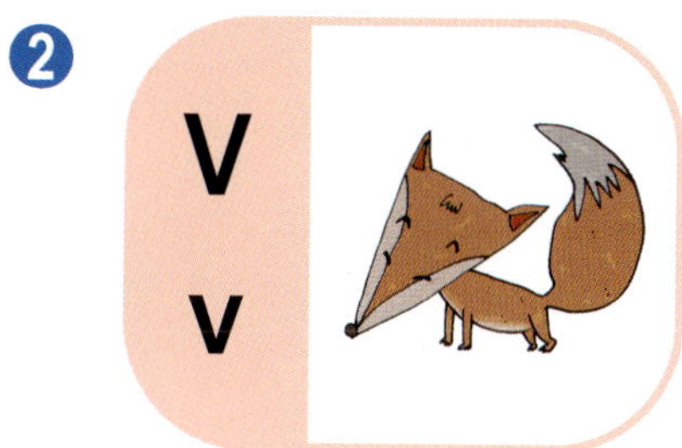  

3   

4   

REVIEW 3

Circle and complete the words.

1  u / t

__U__ n c l e

2  v / w

__ i g

3  w / y

__ e l l

4  x / z

f o __

5  s / y

__ e a

6  v / u

__ e s t

7  t / x

__ i g e r

8  s / z

__ o o

Write the letter in the correct box.

Tt	Xx	Yy	Ww
Xx	Tt	Yy	Ww

1 si [x]

2 [ ] olf

3 bo [ ]

4 [ ] ree

5 [ ] ak

6 [ ] awn

7 [ ] ig

8 [ ] iger

Listen and circle the beginning letters. **track 49**

1 Rr Bb Kk Xx

2 Qq Mm Ii Ff

3 Zz Jj Uu Aa

4 Hh Pp Dd Nn

5 Oo Ll Ss Ee

Listen and circle the T or F. `track 50`

TEST

Match the pictures with the same beginning sounds.

1

2

3

4

5

Circle the picture with a different beginning sound.

Find the correct letter for the picture.

1 
  ⓐ Oo   ⓑ Qq   ⓒ Aa

2 
  ⓐ Nn   ⓑ Kk   ⓒ Mm

3 
  ⓐ Ee   ⓑ Ii   ⓒ Uu

4 
  ⓐ Bb   ⓑ Gg   ⓒ Aa

5 
  ⓐ Dd   ⓑ Pp   ⓒ Ff

Look, circle and write the letters.

Answer Key

Review 1

p.38

 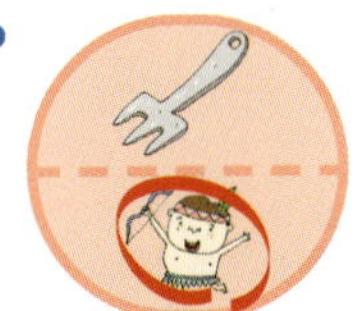

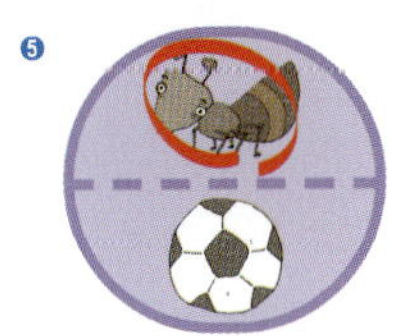 

p.39

❶H ❷c ❸a ❹G ❺B ❻d

p.40

❶F ❷i ❸C ❹d ❺H

p.41

❶c ❷d ❸g ❹h ❺e ❻a

Review 2

p.72

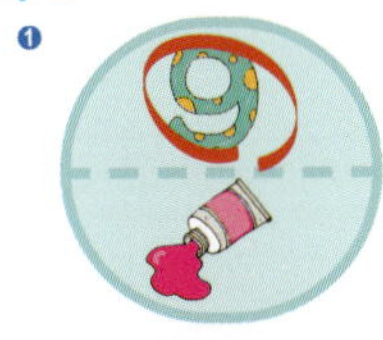 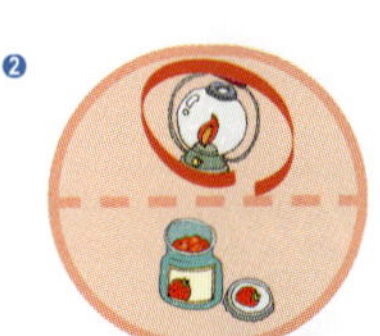

p.73

❶m ❷o ❸J ❹q ❺N ❻R

p.74

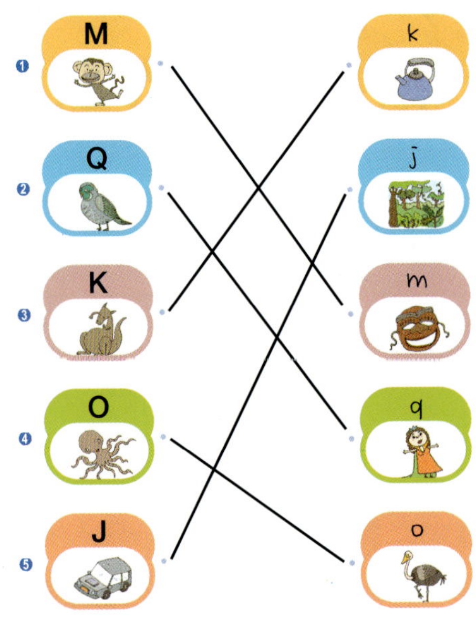

p.75

❶o ❷p ❸l ❹r ❺n ❻l
❼q ❽k

Review 3

p.106

p.107

①  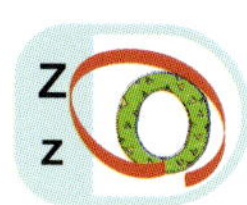 

② 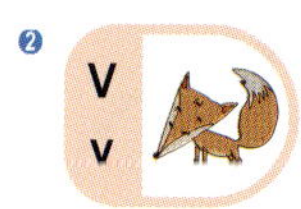  

③   

④   

p.108

❶ u ❷ w ❸ y ❹ x ❺ s ❻ v
❼ t ❽ z

p.109

❶ x ❷ w ❸ x ❹ t ❺ y ❻ y
❼ w ❽ t

Test

p.110

❶ Kk ❷ Ff ❸ Zz ❹ Pp ❺ Ee

p.111

❶ F ❷ F ❸ T ❹ F ❺ F ❻ T
❼ T ❽ T

p.112

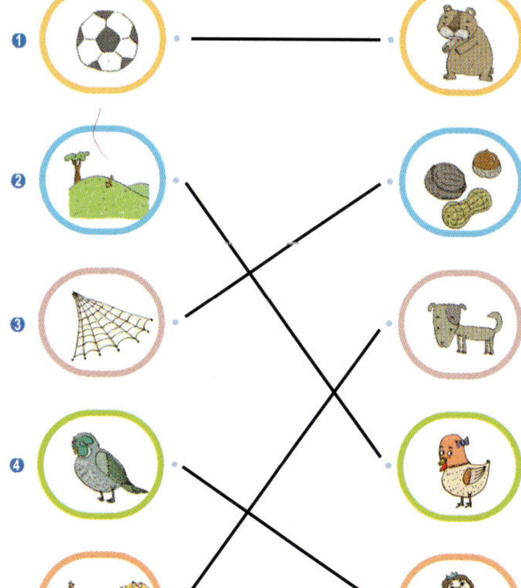

p.113

❶ seal ❷ nine ❸ horse ❹ quilt ❺ big

p.114

❶ ⓐ ❷ ⓒ ❸ ⓑ ❹ ⓒ ❺ ⓑ

p.115

❶ Aa ❷ Oo ❸ Kk ❹ Ii
❺ Cc ❻ Ll ❼ Ff ❽ Pp

Color the right partner letters.

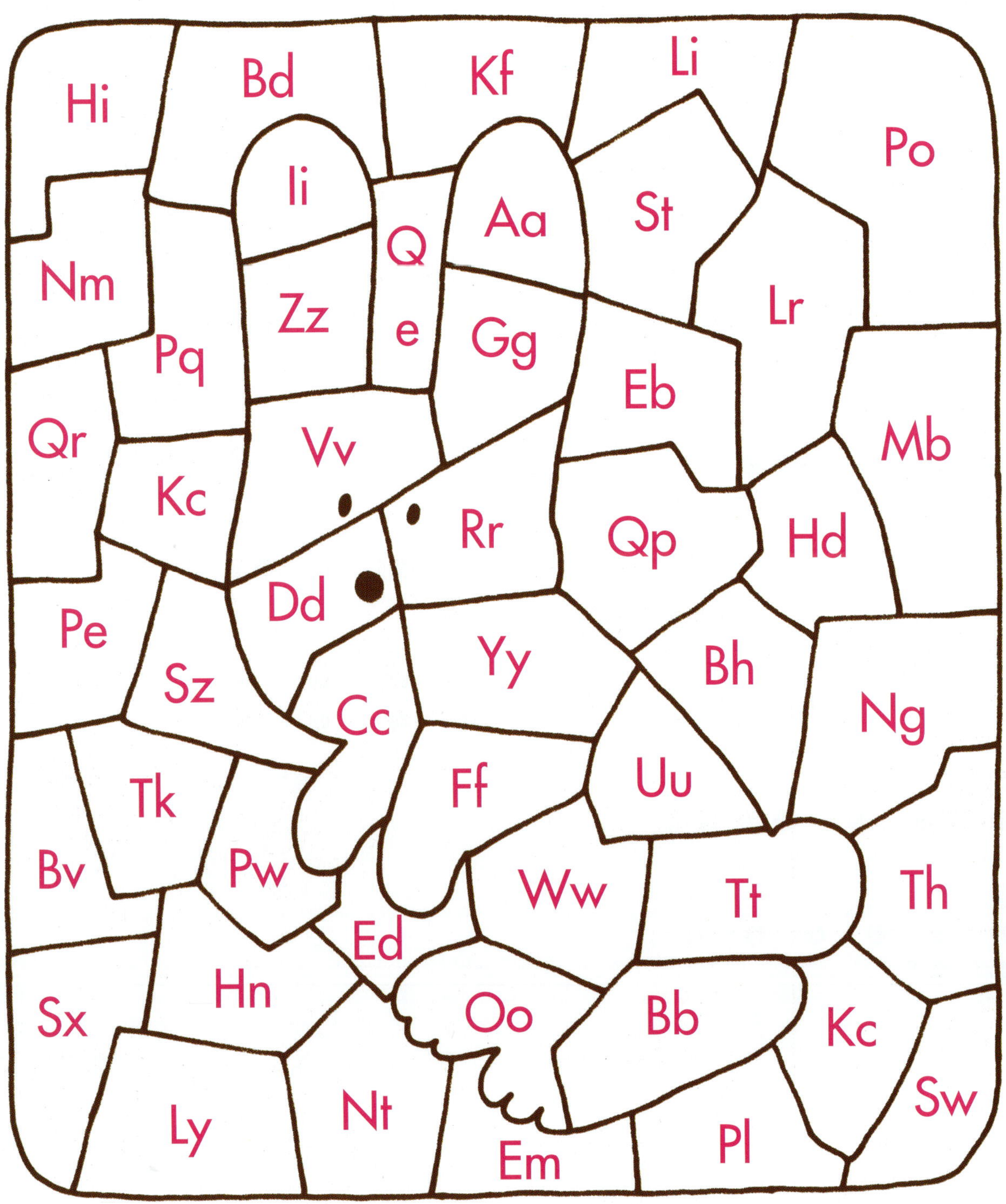

Flash Cards

Eskimo	candy	big	ant
elephant	dirty	ball	apple
elevator	dog	cat	animal
fork	duck	crown	bear

Flash Cards

frog

full

gorilla

guitar

garden

hen

horse

hill

Indian

iguana

insect

jeep

jungle

jam

kangaroo

kick

ostrich	nut	monkey	kettle
pink	net	make	lion
pig	octopus	mask	lamp
paint	omelet	nine	log

Flash Cards

ugly	sea	rabbit	quail
uncle	twins	rose	queen
umbrella	tiger	seal	quilt
vulture	tree	sing	rocket

Flash Cards
ZOO

zero	yak	wig	vane
zebra	yell	six	vest
	yawn	fox	wolf
	zoo	box	wet